Game Cookery

Contents

Game Cookery

Preparation, Freezing, Cooking and Recipes of Game

Published by
Countryside Publications Limited,
School Lane, Brinscall, Near Chorley, Lancashire.
Telephone 0254 831172

Printed by
Tamley-Reed Limited.

ISBN 0 86157 002 2

Introduction

A cookery book with a difference, directed at the housewife or the sporting gun who likes to utilise the contents of the mixed bag to the full. The reader is led, through well tried recipes compiled by the Wildfowlers Association of Great Britain and Ireland, through selected menus created by Jean Bond, to the delight of sharing with friends in the enjoyment of a complete evening at home. The section on freezing provided by Cordon Bleu, the freezer specialists, helps to make sure that no dish will ever be out of season.

Christopher Martin.

Acknowledgments

Grateful thanks are extended to the following;

The Wildfowlers Association of Great Britain and Ireland (W.A.G.B.I.) who supplied all the main recipes which have been written, tried and tested by their members. The freezer sections were all supplied by Cordon Bleu, the largest independent food retailer in Britain. Also Mrs. Jean Bond for her menu planning section and her excellent accompanying recipes.

Preparation

Plucking

When the bird has been hung for the required time it must be plucked. A large paper sack of the stiff variety will be a boon when engaged in plucking the bird. Place the bird in the sack and start with the wings then the neck, working down to the tail Pluck out the feathers away from the bird. Great care must be taken to avoid tearing the skin, especially over the breast. The longer the bird has been hung the more easily it will tear. Remove all down by burning or singeing with an open flame, but do not burn the skin.

Skinning

Some people maintain that it is far easier to skin than pluck a bird, particularly a goose. This can be done through a cut on the front or back. Sometimes only the muscles of the breast and legs are used rather than the whole carcase. When skinned, wrap the whole body in a 'caul' —this is a fatty membrane which any butcher will produce if you give him warning. The skin it makes when cooked is crisp and delicious.

Drawing

If this is the first time you have drawn and cleaned a bird and are a little squeamish over this then wear a rubber glove. As you gain more experience then you will probably dispense with this. Place the bird on the table and cut off the head at the top of the neck. Place the bird breast down and slit down the neck and pull away the loose skin; do not cut it off. Pull out the windpipe and crop, removing the neck close to the spine. Make a short cut between tail and vent and insert two fingers inside the bird. Hold the bird firmly with the other hand and draw out the intestines; make sure the heart, gizzard, liver and gall-bladder are removed. Try not to break the gall-bladder. If you have broken it make sure you wash the inside thoroughly, and dry afterwards with a cloth. Retain the liver, heart, neck and gizzard. Split and clean the gizzard in cold water; keep these for making your stock or gravy.

Trussing

If the bird is to be stuffed this is done before trussing by placing the stuffing in the loose skin from the neck, pressing it down well into the body of the bird. Fold the skin from the neck smoothly under the back of the bird, which should be breast side up, and fold the ends of the wings backwards and under to secure this. Press the legs down into the sides. Thread a trussing needle with thin string and pass this through one wing joint, through the body, out at the top far leg, back on the near side. Tie the string firmly. Thread the needle again and pass the string through the back of the bird beneath the drumsticks, through both drumsticks and then tie the string.

N.B. If you do not have a trussing needle, secure the bird with two skewers, one through the wings and pinning the neck flap to the body, the other passing through the drumsticks.

To Joint a Bird

Slit the skin round the junction of the legs and body and pull the legs outward and downwards so that the thighs break. The legs can then be separated from the body. These may be left whole or divided into thighs and drumsticks. The wings are cut, taking a line from the breast bone downwards to include a slice of the breast. The breast is then separated from the back and cut in half lengthwise.

Hanging of Game

Game is primarily hung to make the meat more tender, the length of time anything may be hung depends on your own personal taste. If you prefer your meat tender but with a gamey flavour, the hang for a longer period of time. For those who require fresher tasting meat but slightly tougher, then shorter hanging times are advised.

Most game birds are hung by the neck, the exception being sometimes young grouse, then it is advisable to hang by the feet as in young birds the neck cannot support the body weight during hanging. Hares are hung by the hind feet. All game should be hung in a well ventilated fly-proof, shaded place. If you overhang game then discolouration of the flesh will occur.

The following table is only a guide to the length of time game should be hung. In warmer weather game should be hung for a shorter period of time. In frosty or cooler weather game may be hung longer.

DAYS

	1	2	3	4	5	6	7	8	9	10	11	12	13	14
Blackcock		●	●											
Capercaillie							●	●	●	●	●	●	●	●
Duck (Wild)	●	●												
Grouse		●	●	●	●	●	●	●	●					
Goose (Wild)	●	●	●	●										
Hare	●	●	●	●	●	●	●							
Pigeon	●													
Partridge	●	●	●	●	●	●	●	●	●	●				
Pheasant	●	●	●	●	●	●	●	●	●	●	●	●	●	●
Quail	●	●												
* Rabbit														
* Snipe	●	●	●	●										
* Venison			●	●	●	●	●	●	●	●	●	●	●	●
* Woodcock	●	●	●	●										

*   Do not hang rabbit.
*   If snipe are to be cooked with the entrails in then care must be taken not to overhang. The same applies to woodcock.
*   Venison. The length of time for hanging depends on the condition of the animal.

Freezing

Freezing Game

Although certain aspects of freezing game are similar to poultry there is one major difference. Whereas poultry can be frozen soon after killing the taste of game is improved by being hung. It is essential that all game is hung before freezing, as if it is hung after thawing the flesh will turn bad. The length of time game is hung varies according to individual preference and also the weather, the average time being 7-10 days, longer in frosty climate. However, whatever the time chosen, game that is to be frozen should be hung for one day less than game to be eaten fresh. This is because some maturing takes place while game is de-frosting. Frozen game should be thawed thoroughly, preferably in a fridge, and cooked as soon as it is defrosted.

Thawing Game

Remove from freezer and thaw overnight in a cool place, ideally a fridge; the bird can then be stuffed before cooking if wished. Older birds can be marinaded after thawing. Pre-cooked dishes should be re-heated in a tightly lidded cooking vessel in a slow oven, basting regularly as soon as sauce is thawed for approximately 40 minutes.

Preparation for the Freezer

It is possible to freeze game whole, without plucking or drawing. However the process of plucking and drawing once the game is thawed becomes a messy and unpleasant one. It is preferable to pluck, draw and dress the bird before freezing, best results are obtained if the bird is kept as cool as possible until you reach home. The bird should then be hung as required and plucked. Then as much shot as possible should be removed from the bird. After drawing, the cavity should be washed and drained and the body not washed but wiped over with a damp cloth. The wing and leg bone should be overwrapped with foil and the bird should then be double wrapped in cellophane or foil and placed in a polythene bag. As much air as possible should be expelled, and the bag should then be tied or sealed, labelled and frozen.

If the bird is frozen jointed, each cut should be double wrapped and then placed in a polythene bag. Stock can be made from the carcass and frozen in ice-cube trays for future use. Double wrapping is important as it will prevent 'Freezer burn' which impairs quality. Game is best frozen raw and unstuffed. Game cooked before freezing should be casseroled to prevent drying out. Such dishes should be frozen in containers with headspace. Giblets must be packed and frozen separately.

Individual Freezing

GIBLETS
To prepare for freezing they should be washed, dried and chilled, packed in a bag to remove air.
To thaw—in the fridge for 2 hours.

GROUSE
Best months for freezing August to October.
Pluck, draw and wrap separately in foil, place a brace in a polythene bag, expel air and freeze. If freezing grouse in casserole form freeze in containers or strong polythene bags.

HARE AND RABBITS
Rabbits available for freezing all year .
Hare—best time for freezing August to February.
Both should be opened and bled as soon as possible, the shot wounds cleaned, and then hung (if required for cooking the hares blood should be collected and frozen in a suitable container). Skin and eviscerate, wash and drain cavity, and wipe the carcass with a damp cloth. These animals should be frozen, cut into joints, and each joint should be packed separately, taking care to expel all air. The joints can then be packed together in usable quantities in a moisture and vapour proof container.

Rabbit and hare can be frozen whole, but join-ting before freezing means a significant reduc-tion in thawing time.

To thaw—

Hare —Whole 24 hours at room temperature
   —Joints 3-4 hours

Rabbit—Place in a fridge overnight, remove and leave covered at room temperature for 1-2 hours before cooking.

PARTRIDGE

Best time for freezing September to January.

As these birds are small, to ensure enough for a good meal, freeze 2 brace (4 birds) in one large polythene bag. Hang birds in their feather without being drawn for the period required, or if the taste of fresh game is pre-fered the birds can be frozen as soon as the body is cool, plucked and drawn.

PÂTÉ

Freeze in rectangular dishes covered with a piece of foil and wrapped in a polythene bag. Pâté should be thawed for 5-6 hours, or over-night in a fridge. Storage time depends on in-gredients and if pork, bacon or garlic is used this reduces the storage time to a month to 6 weeks.

PHEASANT

Best months for freezing, October, November, December and January.

ROAST PHEASANT

When cool cover the breast with gelled juices and freeze wrapped in foil or polythene. Allow to thaw for 5 hours or overnight in a fridge.

PIGEONS

Peak time for freezing is May and June.
To freeze, pluck, remove shot and clean. Place in a polythene bag, remove air, seal and freeze. As these birds are also small it is worth basing catering on one pigeon per person. Thaw in bag in fridge 5 hours per pound or 2 hours per pound at room temperature.

QUAIL

As for snipe and woodcock, do not draw.

SNIPE

Best months for freezing October to December.
As snipe is so small it is not drawn before freezing or cooking. Pluck and strip any skin from the neck and head; the head should then be twisted round and the beak skewered through the wing pinions with needle and string. Secure the legs close to the thighs.

VENISON

Best time for freezing September to November.
If you are not used to large size jointing, then

venison is difficult to prepare and is normally the work of a butcher. However, if you are doing it yourself, be-head and bleed, then skin and eviscerate the animal, wash the interior with cold water. The exterior should simply be wiped with a damp cloth. Prop open the stomach to allow good air circulation and hang in a cold place (ideally just above freezing temperature), scrape off any of the damp sticky substance that may have formed on the outside and dry it well. Rub with flour to keep the surface dry. Cut into joints and wrap well in foil, then place into a polythene bag. It is important to wrap the meat well, as it is a strong meat and this will prevent any cross smells occurring in the freezer.

WILD DUCK

Best months for freezing September to January.

Duck should be hung and cooled, and the oil glands should be removed. Pluck and draw duck and pack giblets separately. Pack in bag, remove air, tie securely, label and freeze. To thaw — 3-4 lbs. duck will need to be left overnight to thaw or 4 hours at room temperature.

WOODCOCK

Best months for freezing October to December.

Though woodcock is a larger bird it should be prepared for the freezer in the same way as snipe. Do not draw and truss as for snipe.

Storage Table

	Storage time in months											
	1	2	3	4	5	6	7	8	9	10	11	12
Capercaillie						●						
Duck				●	●	●						
Giblets		●										
Grouse						●	●	●				
Hare & Rabbit						●	●	●				
Partridge						●	●	●				
Quail						●						
Snipe						●						
Venison										●	●	●
Woodcock						●						

20

Recipes and Menus

Capercaillie

At their best in November and December, these birds should be hung for at least two weeks. Young birds have feet that are supple and the legs are smooth and pliable. The feathers on the breast and under the wings are downy. In older birds the legs are scaly. Capercaillie may be treated in much the same way as grouse. If the bird seems likely to be too 'high', place an onion and some milk inside and leave to stand for 2-3 hours. Throw away onion and milk before cooking. If the birds are young they may be roasted, otherwise it is much better to casserole them. Do not use the gizzard with the other giblets as it often has an unpleasant flavour.

Casserole of Capercaillie

Draw and truss the bird and tie bacon rashers round it. Brown the bird in the hot fat. Place the bird in a casserole and pour the cream over. Cover and cook slowly for 2-2½ hours, basting every half hour. Cook the giblets, omitting the gizzard, in stock and remove. Mince the liver. Add the pan juices, liver and jelly to the stock. Thicken with the flour and cook for about ten minutes. Adjust seasoning. The gravy may be poured over the bird or served separately.

1 Capercaillie
5 rashers of fat bacon
1 pt. cream
1 dessertspoon red currant jelly
½ pt. game stock
Giblets
2 heaped tablespoons flour
Seasoning
Bacon fat

Menu

Country Paté

—

Cauliflower Soup

—

Casserole of Capercaillie
Braised Celery
Broccoli Tossed Salad
Baked Jacket Potatoes

—

Lemon Syllabub

—

Cheese — Biscuits

—

Coffee   Sweetmeats

Country Pâté

Excellently flavoured, this paté slices particularly well. To freeze, cut into individual slices and "open freeze" for about 1 hour. When frozen place the slices in a plastic bag. When required the slices will be able to be individually taken out of the bag. Thaw 1 to 3 hours at room temperature.

1 lb. (400g.) pork sausage meat
1 Egg
2 oz. (50g.) fresh white breadcrumbs
1 medium sized onion
1 level teaspoonful dried sage
1 large baking apple
Salt
Pepper

Method
1. Place sausagemeat, breadcrumbs, finely diced onion, peeled and grated apple, sage, salt and pepper into a large mixing bowl. Add beaten egg.
2. Mix very well together, preferably with the hands until of an even texture.
3. Place into a lightly greased and bottom lined loaf tin and bake Reg 4 or 350°F (180°C) for 1–1¼ hours.
4. Allow to go cold in the tin before carefully releasing from the sides with a knife and removing.

Serving
Serve individual portions on a lettuce leaf or sprig of watercress accompanied perhaps with a slice of salami. Garnish with a wedge of tomato and a little parsley. Two teaspoons of potato salad on the plate is a nice addition. Arrange small triangles of toast to serve with the paté.

Note
Do not be surprised at the use of pork sausage meat in this recipe; it gives an excellent result.

Cream of Cauliflower Soup

Method

1. Divide cauliflower into sprigs and wash.
2. Toss sprigs in melted butter in pan 3 to 4 minutes.
3. Make stock and add to cauliflower. Season and bring to boil. Simmer with lid 45 minutes or until cauliflower is soft.
4. Sieve or liquidise in a blender. Add milk.
5. Return soup to pan — heat — remove from light and add yolk of egg and cream. Serve hot garnished with chopped parsley.

1 small to medium sized cauliflower
1 oz. (25g.) margarine
$\frac{3}{8}$ pt. (250ml.) milk
1 egg yolk
1 tablespoon cream or top of milk

Stock
1 pt. (500ml.) water stock
2 chicken stock cubes

Lemon Syllabub

Method

1. Grater rind and squeeze juice of lemon into a bowl. Add sugar, wine or sherry, and cream.
2. Whisk together until mixture becomes quite thick. Spoon into individual dishes and leave in a cool place.

Note

The syllabub is better made the day before it is required.

1 Lemon
3–4 oz. (75 to 100g.) castor sugar
$\frac{1}{4}$ pt. (125ml.) sweet Spanish white wine or sherry
$\frac{1}{2}$ pt. (250ml.) double cream

Duck with Ginger

The duck should be cooked lightly in butter in the oven and seasoned with the salt, pepper, herbs and ginger, for about 1 hour. When cooked carve the ducks and serve with a baked apple stuffed with raisins and cloves and redcurrant jelly. Make a sauce to serve with the ducks from the juices in the dish they have been cooked in, adding the Port wine and orange juice and a little salt. Boil gently for a minute.

2 cooked wild duck
$\frac{3}{4}$ teaspoonful of ground ginger
Mixed herbs, salt and pepper
$1\frac{1}{2}$ glasses of Port wine
Juice of a large orange

Roast Duck with Tarragon

Clean and prepare duck. Salt and pepper both inside and out. Mix $\frac{3}{4}$ of the chopped tarragon with the butter and place inside the duck. Truss in the usual way. Sprinkle the remaining chopped tarragon on the outer skin. Roast in pre-heated oven, Gas mark 4-5 or electric 350°-400° for approximately $1\frac{1}{2}$ hours or until just cooked.

1 duck, 4-4$\frac{1}{2}$ lb. (or 2 mallard)
1 level teaspoonful chopped tarragon
$\frac{1}{2}$ pt. brown sauce (see recipe)
$\frac{1}{4}$ pt. red wine
2 sprigs fresh tarragon
2 oz. butter

When cooked, remove duck from roasting pan and allow to cool. Meanwhile remove excess grease from roasting pan, saving the duck juices, add the brown sauce, red wine and the fresh–picked tarragon leaves and season to taste. Allow to simmer for 5 minutes. Carve the duck and present with the sauce poured over.

Brown Sauce

Chop the onion, carrot and celery into rough cubes. Melt fat in a saucepan, add the chopped vegetables to the pan and fry gently for 2-3 minutes. Add flour and cook for a further minute then gradually stir in stock and tomato purée. Bring to the boil, stirring continually. Simmer until sauce has reduced by a third. Strain and season to taste.

1 oz. lard or dripping
1 oz. flour (plain)
Salt and pepper
1 onion
1 stick celery
1 teaspoonful tomato purée
Bayleaf, thyme, parsley – a pinch of each
1 carrot
$\frac{3}{4}$ pt. brown stock made from duck giblets

Canard Sauvage Matinale

Clean and pluck duck, singe off all remaining down. Wipe the flesh clean. Do not wash. Salt and pepper the duck inside and out. Place the half apple inside the body cavity and truss. Roast for approximately $\frac{3}{4}$ hour – 1 hour in pre-heated oven 5 or 375°.

Remove duck from roasting tray, untie trussing strings and prepare for serving, either carved or quartered. Take roasting tray and skim off most of the fat. Put tray over moderate heat and stir in the flour and cook for one minute, gradually adding the stock and red wine, half a bay leaf and thyme. Cook slowly for 5 to 10 minutes.

Strain into another saucepan, add sliced glazed mushrooms and whole glazed onions. Season to taste. Coat the prepared duck and sprinkle with chopped parsley. Serves 4.

1 wild duck approximately
3½ lb. (hung for 24 hours)
4 oz. button mushrooms
(glazed) (see recipe)
4 oz. button onions (glazed)
Salt, pepper, half bay leaf,
pinch of thyme
¼ pt. red wine
½ pt. duck stock (made from giblets)
1½ oz. plain flour
½ an apple

To Glaze Onions and Mushrooms

Peel and wash onions or mushrooms. Put in saucepan, barely cover with water and add a pinch of salt and $\frac{1}{2}$ oz. butter. Cook on moderate heat until water has evaporated then gently toss in the residue until a sheen is obtained.

Salmis de Canard Sauvage

Roast the birds and while they are being roasted put the chopped shallots, the herbs, etc. in a small saucepan with the white wine, and simmer gently till reduced to about $\frac{1}{3}$. When the birds are nearly done, carve them carefully, removing all flesh from carcase. Place the pieces of duck in a saucepan with the brandy and set alight. When the brandy is burnt out add a little Espãgnole sauce, cover with a lid and keep warm. Chop up the bones or pound them in a mortar and add to the wine and shallots, mixing well. Add the remaining Espãgnole sauce, stir well and simmer gently and skim carefully. Cook for about 20 minutes. Five minutes before serving, strain half the sauce over the pieces of duck and place the saucepan over a slow fire, but on no account should the sauce be allowed to boil. Remove the remainder of the sauce from the fire, add a few small pieces of butter, not quite 1 oz. altogether, and strain over the birds. Garnish with the cooked mushrooms, a few sliced truffles and *croûtons* of fried bread.

1 or 2 wild duck
1 gill of white wine
1 gill of Sauce Espãgnole
3 or 4 shallots
½ lb. mushrooms
A few truffles (optional)
1 liqueur glass of brandy
1 bay leaf
A sprig of thyme
Salt and pepper

Menu

Tomatoes Farcies

—

Celery Soup

—

Salmis De Canard Sauvage
French Fried Potatoes
Glazed Apples
Peas, Braised Celery

—

Stuffed Peaches
Fresh Cream

—

Cheese — Biscuits

—

Coffee   Sweetmeats

Tomatoes Farcies (Stuffed tomatoes)

Method
1. Prepare tomatoes by wiping. With tomatoes turned stalk end down, cut a "lid" off each rounded end.
2. Scoop out insides with a teaspoon and sieve. Reserve any sieved flesh and juice.

Filling
1. Place rice in boiling salted water. Boil 12 minutes exactly then sieve and rinse under cold running water. Drain well then place in a bowl.
2. Shred flesh of pepper finely (discard core and seeds) and add to rice, together with pineapple, sultanas and onion. Mix well.

French Dressing
1. Place all ingredients in a screw-topped jar and shake.
2. Add 1 tablespoon well shaken French dressing to rive filling mixture to coat all the grains, together with 1 tablespoon reserved sieved tomato flesh. Mix well. Add more of each with care. Excess dressing should not be visible.
3. Pack filling firmly into each tomato shell, allowing a little to come above the top.
4. Replace lids at an angle on top of each.

Filling
4 fairly large red tomatoes
4 oz. (100g.) patna rice
1 finely diced onion
2 tablespoonsful sultanas or.
raisins
2 drained and finely chopped pineapple rings
½ red or green pepper
2 oz. (50g.) shrimps (peeled)
– optional
French dressing
1 tablespoonful vinegar (malt)
3 tablespoonful corn or salad oil
2 teaspoonful cold water
1 pinch mustard
1 good pinch sugar
1 good pinch salt
1 good pinch pepper

Serving

Serve 1 tomato per person with lettuce for garnish, and perhaps a wedge of hard boiled egg. Slices of salami can also be served. Any extra rice salad can be served in a separate dish along with either the tomato starter or the main course.

Celery Soup

Method

1. Cut celery stalks and leaves finely after thoroughly washing. Finely dice onion and potato. Sauté these vegetables in the melted butter in a pan about 10 minutes.
2. Add stock, salt and pepper and simmer about 45 minutes until vegetables are soft.
3. Either thoroughly sieve or liquidise soup, return to pan to reheat. Check seasoning. Stir in cream just before serving hot.

Serving

Sprinkle chopped parsley or grated cheese on top.
Diced fried bread or toast croutons can be handed round separately.

1 celery, including some leaves
1 large potato
1½ pt. (750ml.) stock or water and 2 chicken stock cubes
¼ pt. single cream or rich milk
1 onion
2 oz. (50g.) butter
Salt, pepper

Glazed Apples

Method

1. Heat orange juice, rind and sugar until sugar has dissolved.
2. Wipe and quarter apples without peeling. Carefully remove cores (must not break) and cook very gently* in the orange syrup until soft but not broken.
3. Place in an attractive dish and serve warm along with the Salmis De Canard Sauvage.

*Note

It is worth watching at this stage because on no account must the apples "fall".

2 teaspoonsful grated orange rind
8 tablespoonsful fresh orange juice
4 oz. (100g.) granulated sugar
4 firm red apples

Stuffed Fresh Peaches

Method

1. Wash peaches, cut in half and remove stones. Enlarge a little by scooping out flesh. Reserve.
2. Crush macaroons or cake into a bowl and add extra peach flesh, the yolks sugar and melted butter. Mix well together. Fill hollows in peaches with this mixture.
3. Place in a buttered dish and bake 20–30 minutes – Reg 4 or 350°F (180°C). Meanwhile make meringue topping by whisking egg whites until very stiff, then whisking in half of sugar, removing whisk and folding in remainder of sugar.

4 large ripe peaches
2 oz. (50g.) macaroons or plain sponge cake
2 egg yolks
1 tablespoonful sugar
2 egg whites
4 oz. (100g.) castor sugar
½ oz. (15g.) melted butter

4. When peaches have been cooking about 15 to 20 minutes, place meringue topping on each and cook another 10 to 15 minutes until meringue is crisp and golden.

5. Serve hot with cream.

Note

When fresh peaches are not to hand halved tinned peaches can be used. Wipe free of fruit juice before stuffing and cook for a little shorter time.

Khoresh-e Fesenjan

One of the most exotic and delicious dishes in Iran is Khoresh-e Fesenjan, and in the northern provinces of Iran, where wild duck are abundant in winter, the dish is particularly popular. It is also occasionally made with wild pheasant or even chicken in place of wild duck, but being a so-called 'garmi' or warming dish it is only served in winter time. But "garmi" or not, you should try it once and decide for yourself.

Wash and prepare the wild duck for frying. Sauté the duck with seasoning in shortening. As an alternative method the duck may be baked in a 350° oven for 45 minutes. Put aside. Sauté the onions in 3 tablespoonsful butter until golden brown. Add tomato sauce and sauté for a few minutes. Add walnuts to the sautéd onions and sauté over a medium fire for about 5 minutes. Stir constantly and be careful not to burn the walnuts. Add water, seasoning, lemon juice and pomegranate syrup. Cover and let cook on a low fire for about 35 minutes. Taste the sauce and if you find it a little sour add sugar. Arrange the sautéd duck in this sauce, cover and let simmer for 20-25 minutes. Serve with chelow (steamed rice). Serves 5-6 people.

$2\frac{1}{2}$ to 3 lb. wild duck (jointed)
5 tablespoonsful shortening
$\frac{1}{2}$ teaspoonful poultry seasoning
1 teaspoonful salt
$\frac{1}{2}$ teaspoonful pepper
1 large onion (finely chopped)
3 tablespoonsful butter
2 tablespoonsful tomato sauce
2 cups walnuts (finely chopped)
$3\frac{1}{2}$ cups of water
$\frac{1}{2}$ teaspoonful cinnamon
2 tablespoonsful lemon juice or 2-3 tablespoonsful Pomegranate syrup*
1 tablespoonful sugar
* (obtainable from Greek or Armenian stores)

Fessen Djan

A ragoût, 3 or 4 soupspoons or more, according to personal taste, to be poured over rice and eaten! This recipe is for ten to fifteen people. Recipes for Persian cooking are rather elastic and cannot be exactly timed—after some experience you can adjust the recipe to your personal taste. This ragoût or stew can be eaten plain with rice or you can incorporate into it duck or fish (as eaten in the north of Iran, Province of Gilan for example), or chicken or meat. When using meat in this stew, cut into squares (1½ in. x 1½ in.) and fry before adding to the stew.

Pluck, clean, wash and dry duck. Fry to a golden colour with butter. Add a little water, cover and cook for about ½ an hour (i.e. cook duck half way). Cut duck up into several dices and put aside to incorporate later and cook with your stew.

All these elements are fried separately and then ground through a machine (not too fine). Add about 1½ litres of pomegranate juice to give a creamy texture. If pomegranates are not available use instead 3 or 4 soupspoons of red currant jelly, the juice of 2 or 3 lemons (to compensate for sweetness of jelly, some water to replace liquid of pomegranate juice).

Leave to cook half an hour very slowly in covered saucepan. Then add a full dessertspoon of tomato paste, salt and pepper. Mix well. Leave to cook very slowly for 3 to 4 hours. If substitutes for pomegranates have been used add the tomato paste to the stew

Stew:
150 gr. of dried walnuts. Use without crushing. Fry slightly with butter.
Two egg plants. [You may substitute 2 apples (peeled, cored and cut into 4 pieces) instead of egg plants which are sometimes difficult to get in Europe]. Peel, cut in half, and put aside to drain. Then fry slightly.
One large onion cut into thin slices and fried in butter to a golden brown.

first with a little water. Leave to cook slowly in a covered saucepan for half an hour, then add the rest of the ingredients. The reason for this is to enable the stew to acquire the proper colour. Pass through a machine to a consistency of a purée. When properly cooked the oil will surface and a certain amount may be removed if too greasy for your taste. The duck is to be added to this stew during the last hour or so of cooking—it must be well cooked but not disintegrated. If stew is sour add a little powdered sugar (depending on pomegranates); if too sweet add a little lemon juice. When cooked the stew is a chocolate brown colour.

Goose Pâté

Mince all ingredients twice and place in a basin in the pressure-cooker; $\frac{1}{2}$ pt. of water in the pressure-cooker is sufficient. Cook contents of the basin for 10 minutes at 15 lb. per square-inch. Cool under cold tap and either remince or pass through the liquidizer. In the latter case a little extra fluid may be required and that in the bottom of the pressure-cooker may be used, or a little sherry. Press the pâté into earthenware pots and when cold seal with fresh melted butter.

Cold raw meat cut from 1 or 2 geese
The same weight of ox liver, fat flank, bacon, liver sausage
1 small onion
1 clove of garlic crushed with salt

Accompaniment

Although wildfowl are much less rich than domestic ducks they are basted and cooked in butter and therefore most of the sauces to be served with them are fruit based to counteract any tendency to greasiness. Many have wine added, but it is important that the gravy or sauce does not mask the flavour of the duck itself.

The heart, liver and neck of the duck or goose should be used to make stock for the gravy. This may be augmented or replaced by chicken or bone stock and if necessary by stock cubes.

The gravy or sauce for the duck or goose is very important. It must have a sharp fruit flavour or a red wine flavour. The basic brown sauce which I use is made by frying sliced onions or shallots in butter to which a little oil has been added. The onion should not be allowed to brown, but when tender, sufficient flour is added to absorb the fat and the pan contents simmered until the flour is cooked. The cold duck stock from which the fat has been removed is then added all at once and the mixture is brought to the boil, stirring all the time. The seasoning can be adjusted to taste and the colour deepened with browning.

Grouse

At their best August to mid-October.
Hang for about 1 week in warm
weather. Young birds have bright eyes,
soft pliable feet and smooth legs.
The tip of the breast bone should
also be soft and pliable. In older birds the feet
are hard and scaly with sharp claws and the
breast bone is hard. Young birds are roasted,
usually cut in half, allowing not less than half
a bird per person, but older birds are better
casseroled or used for pâté or terrine.

Casseroled Grouse

Clean the birds and tie a rasher of fat bacon
round each bird. Heat the butter and oil
together and fry shallots and carrots until they
soften. Add the grouse and brown well all
over. Pour over the brandy and flame. Add
the bouquet garni, wine, stock and seasoning
and cook slowly for 2 hours. Thicken with
the beurre manie and adjust the seasoning.
Sprinkle with chopped parsley and garnish
with lemon butterflies.

2 grouse
2 rashers of fat bacon
2 oz. butter
2 tablespoons oil
4 chopped shallots
2 chopped carrots
Salt and black pepper
1 cup red wine
1 cup game stock
Bouquet Garni
2 tablespoons brandy
Chopped parsley
Lemon butterflies
Beurre Manie

Roast Grouse

Draw and clean the bird. Knead the salt, pepper and lemon juice into the butter and put inside the bird. Tie the bacon round the bird and roast in a hot oven for 25 minutes. Serve with fried breadcrumbs, watercress, slices of lemon and cranberry sauce.

Grouse
1 oz. butter per bird
A squeeze of lemon juice
Salt and black pepper
1 rasher fat bacon per bird

Any cold left-over grouse may be served with the following sauce:

Mix the yolk of eggs with the oil gradually till smooth. Add the vinegar and then the other ingredients and season.

2 egg yolks
1 dessertspoonful olive oil
3/4 dessertspoonful white wine vinegar
1 tablespoon castor sugar
1 tablespoon finely chopped shallot
1 tablespoon finely chopped chives
1 tablespoon finely chopped parsley

Grilled Grouse

Cut the birds in half and wipe the inside with a damp cloth. Season the birds with salt and pepper and brush well with melted butter. Place the birds in a buttered grill pan and grill under a very hot grill for about 8 minutes each side, brushing with more butter when necessary. The birds should not be over-cooked. Serve with maitre d'hotel butter on top of each half.

Very young grouse
Melted butter
Maitre d'hotel butter
Salt and black pepper
Grilled mushrooms
Straw potatoes

Menu

Poisson A La Mornay

—

Tomato Soup

—

Roast Grouse
French Fried Potatoes
Brussel Sprouts
Braised Leeks

—

Gooseberry Fool
Strawberry Sauce

—

Cheese — Biscuits

—

Coffee   Sweetmeats

Poisson à la Mornay

Method

1. Wipe fish and place in buttered casserole dish, dab with small amount butter. Add thin rings peeled onion, bay, salt and pepper and pour over the milk.
2. Cover dish and bake about 20 minutes, Reg 5, 375°F (190°C).
3. When cooked place fish on serving dish, keep warm covered with foil. Discard onion and bay leaf and reserve liquor.

Sauce

1. Melt butter in small pan. Add flour and stir. Gradually add milk and, stirring, bring to boil for 1 minute.
2. Reserve 1 spoonful of cheese and add rest of cheese to sauce. Stir and adjust seasoning. Lastly, add cream. Pour sauce over warm fish.
3. Sprinkle remainder of cheese over the dish and grill until golden brown.
4. Garnish with prawns (or halved and deseeded grapes) and parsley.
5. Serve hot with buttered brown bread.

4 small even sized pieces white fish; e.g. hake, halibut
Few pats butter
½ pt. (125 ml.) milk
½ oz. (15 g.) butter
Salt, pepper
2 oz. (50 g.) grated cheese
Few prawns for garnish
Paprika pepper (optional)
1 onion (very small)
1 tablespoonful cream or rich milk

Cream of Tomato Soup

Method

1. Melt butter in large pan and add finely diced onion, carrot and bacon. Allow to sauté in the butter, keeping the lid on for 10–15 minutes. Shake pan occasionally.
2. Wash and slice tomatoes, taking care not to lose any juice and add to pan. If using cans, open and add.
3. Dissolve stock cubes in water and add bay leaf, mixed herbs, salt, pepper and sugar. Simmer about 1 hour. Vegetables must be tender.
4. After cooking remove bay leaf and sieve all into a bowl, leaving very little to discard.
5. Blend milk with cornflour and add to sieved soup. Return to pan.
6. Bring to boil, serve very hot garnished with chopped parsley. Serve toast croutons separately.

Note

2 lb. tomatoes can be used instead of tomato purée. This soup must be sieved and not liquidised.

$1\frac{1}{2}$ lb. (750g.) fresh or equivalent can of tomatoes
1 large onion
1 large carrot
2 rashers lean bacon

Stock
$1\frac{1}{2}$ pt. (750ml.) boiling water
2 chicken stock cubes
$\frac{1}{4}$ pt. (125ml.) milk

1 bay leaf
Pinch mixed herbs
1 level teaspoon sugar
1 oz. (25g.) butter
1 oz. (25g.) cornflour
Salt, pepper
1 dessertspoon tomato purée (see note)

Gooseberry Fool with Strawberry Sauce

Method

1. Top and tail gooseberries. Wash, then stew in covered pan with sugar and very little water (about 1 tablespoon), taking care not to burn.
2. Sieve, taking care to sieve as much of the cooked gooseberries through as possible. Discard skins. Allow to go cold.
3. Make custard (no sugar used) and stir until cold to prevent skinning.
4. Whisk cream or evaporated milk until thick.
5. Stir custard, then cream into gooseberry purée and mix well together. Pour into serving dish and chill.
6. Decorate with cherries and Angelica.

Note

Evaporated milk can be used when a less rich fool is called for. A Strawberry Sauce is a delicious accompaniment to a Gooseberry Fool made by sieving ½ lb. (200g.) strawberries into a bowl and adding juice of 1 lemon and 3 oz. (75g.) sugar. Leave until sugar has dissolved then stir into ½ pt. (250g.) whisked cream. If liked a dessertspoonful Grand Marnier can be added along with the cream, but is entirely optional.

1 lb. (400g.) gooseberries
fresh or equivalent frozen
4 oz. (100g.) sugar
¼ pt. (125 ml.) cream (or 1
small tin evaporated milk)
Custard
½ pt. (250ml.) milk
½ oz. (15g.) custard powder

Salmis of Grouse

Half roast the grouse. Joint them and put in a casserole. Crush the giblets with the juices, add wine, stock, seasoning, juice and zest of lemon and the mushrooms. Pour this sauce over the birds and cook in a moderate oven for about 20 minutes. Make a beurre manie of the butter and flour and stir this into the sauce. Sprinkle with chopped parsley and garnish with lemon butterflies.

2 grouse
1 cup of dry white wine
1 cup of concentrated game stock
4 oz. button mushrooms
1 lemon
Salt and black pepper
Chopped parsley
1 oz. flour
1 oz. butter

Braised Grouse

Joint the birds and fry in the bacon fat until brown. Place the onion and celery on the bottom of a casserole and the bird on the vegetables. Pour in enough stock just to cover the bird and cook slowly for 2 hours. Thicken with the beurre manie and adjust the seasoning.

2 grouse
2 onions
Half a head of celery
2 oz. bacon fat
Beurre Manie
Game stock

45

Hare

There are two types of hare: the English Brown Hare and the Scotch or Blue Hare. The Brown Hare is larger and altogether better. A full grown hare will serve up to eight persons; a leveret (young hare) will serve up to five or six people. Young hares have small white teeth, smooth coats and soft ears. The claws should be hidden beneath the fur and the small nut on the paw well developed. With age, the claws, which are then rounded and rough, project slightly; the teeth become long, yellow and irregular and the cleft in the jaw more evident. White hairs appear in the muzzle; the slightly wavy coat shows traces of grey, and the ears are tough and dry. Hares cannot be offered for sale between 1st March and 31st July. They are usually hung, head down, for a week or ten days. They should then be skinned, drawn and the blood which collects under the membrane in the ribs should be retained.

Roast Hare

Prepare the hare and stuff it with one of the following forcemeats. Sew up the hare and truss it. Tie slices of fat bacon round the hare. Heat the dripping in a roasting tin, put in the hare, cover and place in a hot oven. Cook for 2 hours, basting well every 20 minutes. When the hare is nearly done, remove the bacon, sprinkle flour on the hare and baste until nicely brown. Remove string from the hare and keep warm. Pour off the fat from the tin apart from 2 dessertspoonful. Add 2 dessertspoonful flour to the fat and cook until brown. Add the stock, juice of ½ lemon and the port and jelly. Boil gently for 5 minutes, stirring all the time, adjust the seasoning, remove from heat and add the blood of the hare. Sit the hare upon the serving dish, place a little parsley in its mouth and half a stuffed olive in each eye socket. Garnish round the dish with watercress and lemon slices. Hand the gravy separately.

1 young hare
½ lemon
1 wineglass port
2 dessertspoons flour
Forcemeat
6 rashers of fat bacon
1 tablespoon red currant jelly
½ lb. dripping
Seasoning
1 pt. stock

Forcemeats

(1) Anchovy and herbs

Chop all dry ingredients, mix well and bind with orange juice and beaten egg.

1 onion
4 tablespoons fresh bread-crumbs
1 tablespoon parsley
Beaten egg
Seasoning
1 rasher of bacon
1 tablespoon suet
½ tablespoon thyme
½ tablespoon marjoram
Juice and zest of lemon

(2) Herb

Chop all dry ingredients finely, mix well and bind with beaten egg.

6 oz. fresh bread crumbs
1 oz. fat bacon
1 dessertspoon chopped chives
1 teaspoon thyme
Grated rind and juice of
 1 lemon
2 oz. suet
4 shallots
1 dessertspoon chopped parsley
6 fillets anchovy
Beaten egg

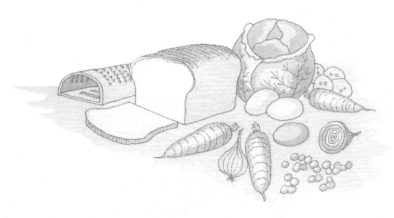

Menu

Stuffed Eggs

—

Chicken Soup

—

Roast Hare
Duchess Potatoes
Courgettes, Braised Leeks
Tossed Salad

—

French Fruit Salad
Fresh Cream

—

Cheese — Biscuits

—

Coffee   Sweetmeats

Stuffed Eggs

To serve 4 allowing two halves per person

1 tin sardines (in oil)
Salt, pepper
4 eggs
2 tomatoes
1 tablespoon cream or mayonnaise
A few crisp lettuce leaves
Cayenne pepper (optional)
Parsley

Method
1. Hard boil eggs by placing in pan covered with cold water. Bring to boil then simmer 8 minutes. Allow to cool in cold water, then shell.
2. With a knife dipped in cold water (to make a clean cut) cut each egg into halves lengthways.
3. Using a teaspoon, scoop out the yolks and place in a bowl. Add salt and pepper and cream or mayonnaise, and mash with a fork.
4. Drain sardines of oil, cut off tails and add 2 sardines to the yolk mixture. Mix well together.
5. Using a teaspoon, pile the mixture back into the egg white shells as attractively as possible. For a special occasion the mixture could be piped using a nylon bag and star savoy tube.

Serving
Serve 2 halves per person on a dry lettuce leaf. Garnish with a sprinkling of cayenne pepper and a piece of parsley on top of the yolks. By the side of the eggs place a quarter of the remaining sardines and a piece of tomato. Serve with thin slices of brown bread and butter.

Alternative fillings instead of sardines.
Allow anchovies to stand 2 minutes in boiling water or cold milk to remove strong salty flavour.

2–3 ozs. (50-75g.) grated cheese
Anchovies
1 tablespoon chopped chives o
spring onions

Cream of Chicken Soup

Method

1. Peel and roughly chop onion and carrots.
2. Melt butter and lightly fry.
3. Add stock, salt, seasoning, bay leaf and parsley. Simmer covered for about 1 hour or until vegetables are soft.
4. Sieve or liquidise, add milk. Reheat and stir in cream just before serving garnished with chopped parsley.

Note

The flavour of this soup can be enhanced by using stock made from bones of a chicken.

2 carrots
1 large onion
½ pt. (250ml.) milk
1 bay leaf
1½ pts. stock made with 2 chicken cubes — or chicken stock (see note)
Salt, pepper
2–3 tablespoonfuls cream or rich milk
Few parsley stalks
1 oz. (25g.) butter

French Fruit Salad

Method

1. Make fruit syrup by squeezing juice of lemon and adding to water and sugar in a pan. Add 2 pieces rind of lemon. Heat gently to dissolve sugar, then allow to cool. Remove rind and discard.
2. Prepare fruit according to type and place a deep layer at the bottom of a suitable serving dish — dust with sieved icing sugar. Repeat in layers of fruit and icing sugar and finish with a dusting of icing sugar.
3. Pour over either the chosen liqueur or fruit syrup. Leave overnight in refrigerator so that

1 lemon
¼ pt. (125ml.) water
2 oz. (50g.) sugar
Fruit in season
Fruit syrup or
2 tablespoons liqueur per pound (400g.) of fruit (see note)

the juices can be drawn from the fruits. Serve with fresh cream and shortbread if liked.

Note
Liqueurs most suitable for fruit.
Grand Marnier with raspberries, pears, peaches and melon.
Brandy with peaches, pears and cherries.
Apricot Brandy with nectarines and apricots.
Punch with cherries, strawberries, plums and blackcurrants.
Maraschino with grapefruit, oranges.
Apricot Brandy apricots, nectarines.

Hare Pâté

Make a marinade by mixing together the oil, wine, brandy, herbs, nutmeg, thyme and crushed cloves. Cut the meat of the hare away from the bones, and marinate the meat for 24 hours. Mince the hare and liver and mix with the port, marinade, blood and seasoning. Line the bottom and sides of a terrine with the strips of fat bacon. Put the mixture into the terrine and place the bay leaves on top. Cover with strips of fat bacon and tin foil. Cook for $2\frac{1}{2}$-3 hours in a moderate oven. Leave for 12 hours before turning out of terrine. Remove bacon strips and bay leaf. Wrap in greaseproof paper and foil and keep in refrigerator for at least a week before using, not forgetting to remove from refrigerator 12 hours before serving.

1 hare plus blood and liver
$\frac{1}{2}$ glass brandy
1 lb. fat bacon strips
1 teaspoon mixed herbs
1 dessertspoon olive oil
2 bay leaves
$\frac{1}{4}$ pt. red wine
2 cloves
1 lb. minced pork
1 teaspoon crushed thyme
6 cloves garlic
Pinch of ground nutmeg
Salt and black pepper

Civet of Hare with Garlic

Joint the hare and marinate for 24 hours in the lemon juice and half the oil. Dry the hare and fry in hot oil until brown all over. Add the marinade, lemon juice, wine, skinned garlic, herbs and seasoning. Simmer for 3 hours. Thicken slightly with beurre manie. Add some of the sauce gradually to the hare's blood and return to the pan. Do not allow to boil. Serve with croûtons rubbed with garlic.

1 hare
1 teacup lemon juice
1 onion
1 dessertspoon chopped fresh herbs
Seasoning
6 tablespoons olive oil
2 glasses red wine
20 small cloves garlic
$\frac{1}{2}$ pt. stock
Beurre Manie

Saddle of Hare

Trim the saddle and place in a deep glass or china dish. Slice the vegetables and put over and round the saddle together with the crushed garlic and herbs. Pour over the brandy and sherry and leave to marinate for 24 hours. Dry the saddle and wrap around with the bacon rashers. Strain the marinade, place the vegetables on the bottom of a casserole and set the saddle on top. Pour over the sherry and brandy, baste well and cover. Cook for 1½ hours in a moderate oven, basting frequently. Boil up with stock, add the cream and reduce a little. Thicken with the beurre manie. Remove the saddle from the oven and place on a serving dish. Strain the juices from the casserole into the sauce. Add a couple of spoonsful of the sauce to the blood and return to the pan. Do not allow to boil after the blood has been added. Surround the saddle with the grapes and pour the sauce over.

1 saddle of hare
2 onions
2 cloves garlic
2 glasses sherry
½ pt. stock
2 tablespoons hare blood
Beurre Manie
4 rashers fat bacon
1 carrot
1 tablespoon brandy
Bouquet Garni
½ pt. cream
4 oz. green grapes
Seasoning

Hare Pudding

The 'wings' and legs only may be used for this dish if the back has been taken for another purpose. Cut the hare into medium sized pieces and marinate. Line a pudding basin fairly thickly with $\frac{3}{4}$ of the suet crust. Place the bacon rashers round the sides and across the bottom of the suet crust. Roll the pieces of hare in seasoned flour and place in basin. Add onion, hare, seasoning, jelly and port, and as much stock as necessary. Cover with greased paper and a pudding cloth and boil or steam for 4 hours. Serve in the basin with a napkin tied round, accompanied by redcurrant jelly.

$\frac{3}{4}$ *lb. suet crust*
4 rashers streaky bacon
1 dessertspoon mixed chopped herbs
1 glass port
Seasoning
Hare
1 dessertspoon chopped onion
1 tablespoon redcurrant jelly
Stock

Rable de Lièvre

Joint the hare and marinate for 36-48 hours. Remove the back and spread lightly with mustard. The remainder of the hare may be used for jugging or pâté, etc. Brown the back slowly in hot butter. Add the strained marinade and allow it to reduce to about a third. Pour on the stock so that the meat is just covered. Bring to boil, cover and cook in a moderate oven until tender, about an hour. Place the hare on a serving dish and keep warm. Add the cream, boil for a minute, adjust the seasoning, and strain the sauce. Spoon a little sauce over the meat and hand the rest separately.

1 hare
$\frac{1}{2}$ *pt. cream*
$\frac{1}{2}$ *pt. good stock*
French mustard
1 oz. butter

Jugged Hare

Joint the hare and soak in the marinade for 36 hours. Dry the meat well and fry in the bacon fat. Place the hare in a large earthenware pot or casserole. Slice the carrot and celery and add these to the hare, together with the spices, seasoning, bouquet garni, rind and juice of the orange, 1 cupful of the marinade and enough stock to just cover the meat. Cover the pot tightly and cook in a slow oven for $3\frac{1}{2}$ hours. Place the hare in a serving dish and keep warm. Strain the liquid from the casserole and thicken it with beurre manie until it is the consistency of thin cream. Remove the sauce from the heat and add several spoonsful of the sauce by degrees to the blood. Then pour it back carefully into the pan, together with the port and redcurrant jelly. Pour over the hare and reheat gently, taking care not to allow it to boil. If necessary shake the casserole gently. Do not stir as this will break up the pieces of hare. The sauce should be smooth and rich. Serve with forcemeat balls fried in butter or deep fat.

Hare or legs and 'wings' of hare
2 onions stuck with 3 cloves
1 carrot
1 teaspoon all spice
Rind and juice of 1 orange
1 large glass port
Marinade
Seasoning
2 oz. bacon fat
1 stick celery
5 peppercorns
Bouquet Garni
$1\frac{1}{2}$-2 pt. stock
1 dessertspoon red currant jelly
Beurre Manie
Forcemeat balls

N.B. The essential part of this dish is that, after a long slow cooking, the sauce should be thickened with a blood liaison and enriched with port.

Partridge

At their best in October. Hang from 4 to 8 days according to weather and taste. The grey partridge is generally thought to be better flavoured than the red-legged or French partridge, but is a smaller bird. The legs of young birds are olive coloured and the beak softer and darker in colour than those of old birds, whose legs are silver. Partridges may be cut in half, allowing one half bird per person, but many people can eat a whole bird. If available a vine-leaf tied next to the skin of the bird when cooking will bring out the flavour.

Perdreaux à la Rouennaise

Draw and truss the birds. Heat the butter and brown the birds well all over. Peel and slice the apples, arrange in the bottom of a casserole and sprinkle with the sugar. Pour the butter in which the birds were browned over the apples. Lay the birds on the apples, season and pour the cream over. Cover and cook slowly until tender, $1\frac{1}{2}$-2 hours. Place the birds on a serving dish surrounded by the apples.

2 partridge
$\frac{1}{2}$ pt. cream
1 teaspoon brown sugar
1 lb. cooking apples
2 oz. butter
Seasoning

Grilled Partridge à la Diable

Split the partridge in two and flatten each half slightly. Season and brush the bird with melted butter. Cook under a moderate grill for 4 minutes each side. Brush with melted butter and coat with fresh white breadcrumbs. Finish grilling gently, brushing frequently with melted butter. Arrange partridge on serving dish and garnish with watercress, lemon butterflies and thinly sliced gherkins. Serve sauce separately.

Partridge
Butter
Fresh breadcrumbs
Seasoning
Watercress
Lemon butterflies
Gherkins
Diable sauce

Diable Sauce

Cook the shallots in butter until lightly coloured. Add brandy and reduce to half. Add espagnole and purée. Simmer for 5 minutes. Add chervil, cayenne and Worcester sauce.

½ pt. espagnole sauce
1 tablespoon finely chopped shallots
1 level teaspoon chopped chervil
Cayenne pepper and Worcester sauce to taste
Butter
1 teaspoon tomato purée
1 sherry glass brandy

Menu

Parma Ham and Melon

—

Vegetable Soup

—

Grilled Partridge à La Diable
French Fried Potatoes
Grilled Tomatoes
Peas
Tossed Salad

—

Plum Crumble
Fresh Cream

—

Cheese — Biscuits

—

Coffee   Sweetmeats

Parma Ham with Green Figs or Melon

Method
1. Prepare melon. With a knife cut segments of melon away from peel, then arrange attractively in the shells. Twist a ring of orange on a cocktail stick.
2. Arrange Parma ham by the side of the melon, with perhaps a lettuce leaf and wedge of tomato.

Note
Green figs can be served instead of melon.

Thin slices parma ham (approx 2 slices per person)
4 thin slices melon

Vegetable Soup

Method
1. Prepare vegetables by peeling and chopping. Dice onion finely.
2. Melt butter in pan and sauté vegetables about 10 minutes with lid on.
3. Add stock and simmer about 1 hour or until vegetables are soft, then sieve into a bowl or liquidise.
4. Adjust thickness of soup with the addition of milk. Serve hot garnished with parsley.

1 lb. mixed vegetables (carrot turnip, cauliflower)
1 onion
Stock
1 chicken stock cube
1 pt. (500ml.) boiling water
1 oz. (25g.) butter
¼ pt. (125ml.) milk

Plum Crumble

Method

1. Slit plums with knife, remove stones. Place in pan with butter, sugar and water, cover and simmer about 10 minutes or until fruit is soft.
2. Place fruit in suitable dish. Make crumble topping by rubbing butter into flour and sugar until it resembles fine breadcrumbs. Sprinkle evenly on top of plums and bake about 45 minutes, Reg 4 or 350°F (190°C).
3. Serve with custard or cream. Delicious with ice cream.

Note

Winter crumbles can be made from home bottled fruits or fruits frozen in a freezer.

1½ lb. (600g.) plums
6 oz. (150g.) sugar
½ oz. (15g.) butter
1 tablespoon water
Crumble
6 oz. (150g.) plain flour
4 oz. (100g.) butter
2 oz. (50g.) sugar

Roast Partridge

Clean and truss the bird. Insert a lump of butter worked up with seasoning and a little lemon juice. Tie a vine leaf, if obtainable, and a rasher of fat bacon over the bird and roast in a well buttered tin in a hot oven for 20 minutes. Serve on croûton of fried bread with the pan juices poured over. Garnish with lemon and watercress.

Boiled Partridge-Cold

Season a young bird inside and out and wrap it in vine leaves and fat bacon. Put into boiling water and boil for 35 minutes. Plunge immediately into just enough iced water to cover it, leave long enough to become quite cold but no longer. Serve with a plain green salad.

Casserole of Partridge

Season the birds inside and out. Truss. Fry the bacon and shallots lightly and put in the bottom of a casserole. Fry the birds until brown all over and put on top of bacon and shallots. Fry the mushrooms very lightly and add. Add the stock, cover and cook in a very moderate oven for a further $\frac{3}{4}$ hour. Thicken with the beurre manie.

Partridge
Butter
1 oz. bacon per bird
3 oz. shallots per bird
2 glasses red wine per bird
Seasoning
Beurre Manie
4 oz. button mushrooms per bird
$\frac{1}{2}$ gill stock per bird

Partridge à la Creme

Season the bird inside and out and truss. Fry with the onion in the butter until brown. Cook in a covered casserole in a hot oven for 10-15 minutes. Mix the cream and lemon juice and pour over the bird. Cook for a further 10 minutes, basting frequently.

Young partridge
Butter
3 drops lemon juice
1 small chopped onion
1 cupful cream
Seasoning

Pheasant

Probably the most popular of English game birds. At their best November to January. Hang for one to four weeks according to weather and taste. A young cock pheasant has rounded spurs with no points in its first year; short but pointed when two years old; after that sharp and long. A young hen has soft feet whilst an older bird has hard rough feet. A pheasant will serve 2, 3 or 4 persons depending on its size. Young birds are excellent roasted but it is advisable to casserole an old bird.

Pheasant Normande

Brown the pheasant all over in the butter. Chop the shallots finely, add to the pan and cook until golden. Flame with the brandy and reduce by half. Add the stock, sliced apples, seasoning and bouquet garni and bring to the boil. Cover tightly and cook slowly for an hour. Remove the pheasant, carve and place on serving dish. Strain the liquid and return to the pan with the cream. Bring to the boil and pour over the pheasant.

1 pheasant
2 shallots
2 cox's apples
¼ pt. thick cream
1 oz. clarified butter
1 glass brandy
¼ pt. jellied stock
Bouquet Garni, Seasoning

Roast Pheasant

Draw and truss the bird. Insert half an onion in the bird, also a piece of fat bacon or a knob of butter. Wrap the bird in fat bacon and place in a covered tin, or wrap loosely in foil. Place in a hot oven for 30 minutes, reduce to 350° and cook for about 40 minutes longer depending on the size of the bird. Make a gravy from stock in which the giblets have been cooked.

1 or 2 pheasants
Fat bacon for larding
1 large or 2 small onions

Menu

Avocado Pears

—

Mushroom Soup

—

Roast Pheasant
French Fried Potatoes
Braised Celery
Peas

—

Christmas Apples
Fresh Cream

—

Cheese — Biscuits

—

Coffee   Sweetmeats

Avocada Pears

Method

1. It is essential the avocado pears are ripe. Cradle the pear in the hand when it should be fairly soft to the touch, particularly at the neck end.
2. Cut pear in half lengthways and with a teaspoon remove the stone.
3. Place cottage cheese, chopped chives, shrimps and pineapple into a bowl and mix. Season.
4. Place heaps of filling into the holes in the pears and top each with sprig parsley.
5. Serve garnished with sliced tomato and cucumber and a lettuce leaf. Serve a Vinaigrette dressing separately.

2 ripe avocado pears
Filling
4 oz. (100g.) cottage cheese
Chopped chives or 1 finely chopped onion
2 or 3 oz. (75g.) shrimps or prawns
Salt, pepper
2 rings pineapple (in small pieces)
Vinaigrette dressing

Mushroom Soup

Method

1. Peel carrot and onion and chop into rough pieces. Place in a pan and add celery, milk, bay leaf, salt and pepper.
2. Heat gently, then remove from light and allow to infuse 30 minutes.
3. Peel mushrooms if necessary and finely chop. Very lightly fry for about 3 minutes in a pan in the melted butter.
4. Strain milk into a pan discard vegetables. Add flour to mushrooms, stir well and gradually blend in the milk.

1 pt. (500ml.) milk
1 small onion
1 small carrot
1 celery stalk (optional)
1 egg yolk
1 oz. (25g.) butter
½ oz. (15g.) flour
1 bay leaf
6 oz. (150g.) mushrooms

5. Return to light and gradually bring to boil, stirring. Season well and simmer 2 minutes. Remove from light and add egg yolk.
6. Serve hot with a little chopped parsley on top and accompanied with melba toast (thin slices of baked bread). Add more milk if a thinner soup is required.

Christmas Apples

Method
1. Wipe apples. Remove cores with potato peeler, leaving a hole in centre of each.
2. Make a fruit syrup by boiling together sugar and water.
3. Fill empty cores with mincemeat. *Place apples side by side in an oven proof dish, pour fruit syrup around apples and bake about 30 minutes Reg. 5, 375°F or 190°C, taking care that the apples do not "fall". Serve hot with the fruit juice and custard or cream.

*Use a vegetable knife to cut a line around centre of each apple to prevent "falling" during baking.

4 baking apples of even size
Mincemeat
Fruit syrup
4 oz. (100g.) sugar
¼ pt. (125 ml.) water

Pheasant Soup

Joint the bird and place in a pan with vegetables and herbs. Simmer for 4 to 5 hours. Mince the breast meat, mix with the breadcrumbs, season and bind with the egg yolk. Shape into small balls. Remove the bones and vegetables from the stock, add the meat balls and simmer for 20 minutes. Just before serving, add the cream.

1 old pheasant
2 carrots
$\frac{1}{4}$ pt. cream
2 onions
2 sticks celery
1 egg yolk
1 leek
Bouquet Garni
2 oz. brown breadcrumbs

Pheasant in Red Wine

Chop the shallots and the birds' livers finely, mix together and place in the cavity of each bird. Heat the olive oil and 2 tablespoons of butter in a large thick pan and sauté pheasants gently until they are golden brown. Place the pheasants in a casserole and keep warm. Put red wine and mushroom stalks in the pan and boil until reduced by half. Thicken the sauce with the remaining butter and flour. Sauté the mushrooms and onions, place round the birds and pour the sauce over. Cover the casserole and cook in a moderate oven for $1\frac{1}{2}$-2 hours.

2 pheasants
2 tablespoons olive oil
1 pt. Burgundy
1 tablespoon flour
4 shallots
3 tablespoons butter
8 oz. mushrooms
Seasoning

Pheasant Pâté

Remove all the meat from the pheasant and mince it with the lean pork, half the fat pork and the bird's liver. Add the thyme, crushed garlic, $\frac{1}{2}$ teaspoon salt and pepper. Mix well, add the brandy and beaten egg and mix again. Line a terrine or earthenware casserole with thin strips of fat pork. Press the mixture into the terrine, place the bay leaf on the top and cover with more thin strips of pork fat. Bake at 350° for $2\frac{1}{2}$ hours. When cold remove from terrine and remove bay leaf and pork. Wash and dry terrine and return pâté to it. Pour over aspic or jellied stock made from the pheasant bones.

1 pheasant
1 lb. fat pork
1 egg
1 clove garlic
Pinch of thyme
4 fluid ozs. brandy
$\frac{1}{2}$ lb. lean pork
Aspic or jellied stock
Seasoning
1 bay leaf

Lincolnshire Pheasant

Cut the onion and carrot into cubes and joint the pheasant. Melt the butter in a strong pan and fry the pheasant, onion and carrot lightly until golden. Add the stock and seasoning and simmer for 30 minutes. Add the tomatoes, quartered, and the mushrooms and simmer for a further 30 minutes. Thicken and serve.

1 pheasant
1 onion
$\frac{1}{2}$ lb. mushrooms
4 oz. butter
$1\frac{1}{2}$ pt. stock
1 carrot
4 tomatoes
2 oz. flour
Seasoning

Pheasant à la Creme

Draw and truss the pheasant, reserving the liver. Heat the butter and oil in a large strong pan and brown the pheasant and liver all over. Add the onion and carrot, both finely chopped, the thyme, crumbled bay leaf and seasoning. Cover and simmer for 20 minutes. Pour off the excess fat and flame with the brandy. Add the cream and simmer until the pheasant is tender, approximately 1½-2 hours, but an old bird may need longer. Mash the liver with a little butter and brandy and spread on a slice of decrusted white bread. Place the bird on this. Strain the sauce, correct the seasoning and pour over the pheasant. The sauce should be thick. If necessary add a little arrowroot or, failing this, cornflour but the latter is not as satisfactory.

1 pheasant
4 tablespoons butter
2 tablespoons onion
1 bay leaf
3 tablespoons brandy
½ pt. double cream
2 tablespoons oil
2 tablespoons carrot
¼ teaspoon thyme
Seasoning

Salmis of Pheasant

Place a knob of seasoned butter inside the pheasant and brush butter liberally over the outside of the bird. Roast in a hot oven for 40 minutes. Carve the bird, removing the skin and bone. Place the pheasant slices on a fireproof serving dish and cover with slices of truffle and the mushrooms cooked in butter. Heat the stock in the roasting tin and pour over the pheasant. Cover and keep warm. Chop up the skin and bones of the bird. Cook the bacon and vegetables lightly together in a little butter. Work in a dessertspoonful of flour until cooked. Add the skin, bones and wine, season and simmer for $\frac{1}{2}$ an hour. Strain the sauce, return to the heat and if necessary thicken with a little beurre manie. Flame the brandy and add to the sauce. Pour over the pheasant. Simmer on the cooker for a few minutes or warm in the oven, but do not let the sauce boil.

1 pheasant
$\frac{1}{2}$ cupful stock
2 shallots
$\frac{1}{2}$ carrot
1 stalk celery
Flour
Seasoning
4 oz. mushrooms
1 rasher bacon
A few truffles (if available)
$1\frac{1}{2}$ glasses red wine
Butter
2 tablespoons brandy

Pigeons and Cranberry Sauce

Brown the pigeons slowly in the butter in a casserole. Remove and divide each bird in 2 and cut away backbone and leg joints. (These may be used for soup.) Fry the shallot until golden. Add the flour and stir for several seconds; then pour in stock, seasonings, and allow to boil.

4 pigeons
1 oz. butter
1 finely chopped shallot
1 tablespoon flour
½ pt. jellied stock
Salt, pepper and a sprinkling of mixed herbs
1 small can of cranberry sauce
4 tablespoons double cream

Replace the pigeons and add the cranberry sauce. Cover and cook in a moderate oven for about 2 hours. Remove the pigeons and keep hot. Work the sauce in a liquidiser until smooth. Replace the pigeons in the casserole, pour over the sauce and add cream. Return to oven for a few minutes before serving.

N.B. Fresh cranberries may be used for this recipe if available – 6 oz. fruit and one tablespoon sugar.

Menu

Courgettes Maison

—

Onion Soup

—

Pigeons and Cranberry Sauce
French Fried Potatoes
Boiled Potatoes
Peas, Broccoli, Grilled Tomatoes

—

Bavarois Au Café

—

Cheese — Biscuits

—

Coffee   Sweetmeats

Courgettes Maison

Method

1. Trim each end of courgettes. Cook whole in boiling salted water 5 minutes. Drain and place in cold water to refresh.
2. Remove thin slice lengthways from each courgette, and using a teaspoon take out the flesh, chop and reserve.
3. Skin tomatoes by placing a few seconds in boiling water, take out seeds, chop flesh coarsley and mix with courgette flesh.
4. Melt butter in pan and gently fry diced onion until soft, add the tomato mixture, paprika, salt and pepper. Cook together 2–3 minutes, then stir in shrimps.
5. Place courgettes in buttered dish and fill them with tomato mixture.
6. Prepare Mornay Sauce by melting butter, adding flour then pouring on the milk. Stirring, bring to the boil, then off the light add cheese, (can be thinned by adding more milk if necessary).
7. Pour sauce over courgettes, sprinkle surface with cheese or breadcrumbs and grill until golden.

Serve with thin slices brown bread and butter.

4 medium sized courgettes
4 tomatoes
1 oz. (25g.) butter
1 small onion (finely diced)
1 teaspoonful paprika pepper
Salt, pepper
2 oz. (50g.) shrimps
1 tablespoon grated cheese or breadcrumbs

Mornay sauce
2 oz. (50g.) cheddar cheese
1 oz. (25g.) butter
1 oz. (25g.) flour
½ pt. (250ml.) milk

Onion Soup

Method

1. Peel and slice onions. Lightly sauté in melted butter in a pan. Cook 45 minutes very slowly, with tight lid. Shake occasionally. During last 10 minutes brown onions by removing lid.
2. Add peeled and diced potato, stock and seasoning to taste. Cook a further 30 minutes, simmering only.
3. Sieve or liquidise – check seasoning – reheat for serving hot garnished with parsley.

1 lb. onions
1 oz. (25g.) butter
Salt, pepper
1 large potato
1½ pts. (750ml.) stock made with 2 beef stock cubes

Bavarois au Café

Method

1. Make egg custard in pan (double if possible) by beating egg and sugar with milk and stirring over low light until it thickens. Allow to cool, occasionally stirring.
2. Stir gelatine into strong coffee and heat until dissolved. Cool, then stir into custard along with the liqueur. Whip cream and gradually beat into mixture. Pour into a mould and allow to set. Turn out and decorate with cherries.

Custard
1 egg
½ oz. (15g.) sugar
½ pt. (250ml.) milk

½ oz. (15g.) gelatine
2½ fluid oz. strong black coffee
½ pt. (250ml.) double cream
1–2 tablespoonsful Creme De Curaçao or Tia Maria

Pigeon Pie

Cut the birds into 4 joints: 2 breasts and 2 leg joints. Put the remainder of the carcasses, with a small onion and a carrot, to stew in a little water. This stock can be made into gravy to eat with the pie.

Line the pie dish with slices of steak about 2 inches long and 1 inch across, then lay the pigeons on top, cover with water and season well. Cover with greaseproof paper, simmer in medium oven for 1-2 hours. Remove dish and cover with pie crust. Glaze top with beaten egg, return to hot oven and bake until golden brown. Fill up with gravy when the pie is opened.

5-6 pigeons
8 oz. stewing steak
8 oz. short pastry
Seasoning
A little good gravy

Pigeon and Potato Pie

Cut the breasts into 4 pieces right through the bones. Dip them and the steak in seasoned flour. Peel and slice potatoes, mushrooms and onion. Put ingredients into a pie dish and season. Three quarters fill the dish with hot stock. Cover with pastry, decorate and glaze. Bake in a hot oven until pastry is browned, then lower temperature and cook for about 2 hours until meat is tender. Cover pastry if necessary to prevent over browning. Before serving, fill up with hot stock.

2 breasts of pigeon
¼ lb. stewing steak cut into small pieces
¾ lb. potatoes
4 oz. mushrooms
1 large onion, parboiled
Seasoned flour
Seasoning
Stock
½ lb. rough puff, flaky or short pastry

Pigeon Pâté

Make a marinade of the wine, vinegar, herbs, seasoning and onions. Pour this over the pigeons and leave for 4 days.

4 pigeon breasts
½ pt. red wine
¼ pt. vinegar
Bay leaf
A teaspoon of mixed herbs
A pinch of nutmeg
Seasoning
2 chopped onions

Mince the meat and liver twice, or put through an electric blender. Mix with the sausage meat very thoroughly, add herbs and seasoning to taste. Soak the bread in milk and beat this into the meat.

Meat taken from birds
2 oz. liver
8 oz. sausage meat
8 oz. fat bacon
Seasoning
2 teaspoons chopped parsley and thyme
1 slice bread, remove crusts
Milk

Butter the inside of an ovenware dish or an earthenware terrine and line the base with a few bacon rashers. Fill the dish with the pâté mixture, spread level and cover with remaining bacon rashers. Cover with a buttered paper and a lid, if the dish has one, or alternatively, a piece of cooking foil. Put in the centre of a moderate oven and bake for 2-3 hours.

Keep for 2 days for the full flavour to develop. This pâté will keep well in a deep-freeze for 2 or 3 weeks.

Pigeons in Cider

Place pigeon breasts on bacon rashers in a casserole. Cover with finely shredded onion, add bay leaf and pour over a ½ pt. of cider. Leave overnight and then cook, tightly covered, in a slow oven for about 2 hours. Then add mushrooms, top with a little stock if necessary, and cook for another hour or so until the pigeons are quite tender.

Before serving, remove bay leaf; thicken and season gravy to taste.

4-6 pigeon breasts
2 bacon rashers
1 large onion
½ lb. mushrooms
½ pt. cider
¼ pt. stock
Bay leaf
Seasoning
Flour

Pigeons with Raisins

Cut bacon into small pieces and fry in butter in pan for 2 to 3 minutes. Remove and carefully brown pigeon breasts. Place in casserole with bacon, season and tip over stock which should barely cover. Bring to the boil, cover tightly and cook for about 1½ hours in a moderate oven.

After half an hour add the onions which have been browned in a pan. Soak the raisins in hot water and about 15 minutes before serving, add them to casserole along with the almonds. Really good stock is essential in this recipe to make a nice sauce, and at the end of the cooking time the gravy should be well reduced and sticky.

4 pigeon breasts
4 oz. streaky bacon rashers
2 oz. butter
½ pt. jellied stock
12 small onions or shallots
2-3 oz. raisins
2 oz. blanched and halved almonds

Casserole of Pigeons with Red Cabbage

Salt and pepper the pigeons and leave them to soak in the marinade for 5-6 hours, turning them 3 or 4 times. Dice the pork and, using a heavy casserole, fry in butter until crisp. Dry the pigeons, sprinkle with a little flour and gently brown them all over in the pork fat. Pour over them the warmed brandy and flambé (to burn off excess fat).

Add the strained marinade, the crushed clove of garlic and more seasoning. Cover tightly, putting a piece of kitchen foil between the contents of the casserole and the lid, to prevent steam escaping. Cook in the centre of a slow oven for $2\frac{1}{2}$-3 hours. Serve the birds on a bed of red cabbage with sauce poured over.

2 pigeons
Salt, pepper
2 oz. belly of pork
$\frac{1}{2}$ oz. butter
Flour
4 tablespoons brandy
1 clove garlic
Marinade:
$1\frac{1}{2}$ gills of dry white wine
1 chopped raw carrot
1 chopped raw onion
Bouquet garni

Red Cabbage

Melt butter in saucepan. Peel and core apple, peel onion, chop together with cabbage and add to butter. Add vinegar, sugar, seasoning, and cover tightly. Cook over a low heat for 2 hours, stirring occasionally.

1 oz. butter
1 apple
1 onion
Seasoning
$\frac{3}{4}$ lb. red cabbage
2 tablespoons vinegar
2 tablespoons soft brown sugar

Curried Pigeon

Chop the onion and garlic finely and blend with the curry powder and paste. Fry in the butter, then add chopped tomatoes and pigeon joints. Work in the flour and cook for several minutes. Add the stock, bring to the boil until thickened. Add the rest of the ingredients and simmer steadily for 3 to 4 hours. Serve with boiled rice and side dishes.

3 pigeons – jointed
1 onion
2 cloves garlic
2 tomatoes
1 tablespoon curry powder
1 teaspoon curry paste
1 tablespoon flour
$\frac{3}{4}$ pt. brown stock
1 level teaspoon brown sugar
1 oz. dried fruit
Seasoning
1 tablespoon dessicated coconut
1 tablespoon lemon juice
Bunch of fresh herbs

Goulash

Heat the butter in a pan. Cut meat into neat pieces. Slice onion thinly. Fry meat and onion until pale golden brown, add paprika pepper and other seasoning, tomato pulp, stock and simmer gently for $1\frac{1}{2}$ hours. Add sliced potatoes and cook for another 1-2 hours until the meat and potatoes are very tender. More stock can be added during cooking if necessary, but the mixture should be very thick. Garnish with chopped parsley, and top with sour cream.

4 pigeon breasts
2 oz. margarine or butter
2 sliced onions
Pinch mixed herbs
Parsley
1 teaspoon salt
1 tablespoon paprika pepper
Pinch caraway seeds
$\frac{1}{4}$ pt. tomato pulp
1 lb. potatoes
A little stock or water

Pigeons & Cherries

Heat the butter and oil in a large frying pan. Add the pieces of pigeon and brown lightly. Pour the sherry over. Remove the pigeon from pan and place on a hot dish. Put the garlic and half the drained cherries into the pan. Allow to cook for a few minutes. Blend the cornflour with a little of the drained cherry juice and tomato puree. Add to the sherry mixture in the pan with the rest of the cherry juice and stock. Cook over a moderate heat, stirring well until the sauce has thickened. Put the pigeons back into the pan and add the bayleaf. Cover with foil and a lid and simmer over a low heat for $1\frac{1}{2}$ −2 hours. Arrange the pigeons on a dish with sauce poured over, and garnish with the rest of the cherries, slices of orange and watercress.

2 oz. butter
1 tablespoon cooking oil
2 pigeons, quartered
2 tablespoons dry sherry
1 clove garlic—crushed
14 oz. can of black cherries
$\frac{1}{2}$ oz. cornflour
1 teaspoon tomato puree
$\frac{1}{4}$ pt. stock
1 Bay leaf
1 orange—sliced
Small bunch watercress

Quail

Need little or no hanging. In this country quail are uncommon in the wild, but are reared on game farms and on sale, ready prepared, from a delicatessen or poulterer. Allow one bird per person as a 'starter' and two for a main meal.

Casserole of Quail with grapes

Truss the birds. Rub with salt and pepper and wrap each bird first in a vine leaf and then in fat bacon. Sauté the birds in the melted butter for 10 minutes. Remove the birds from pan and arrange in heat-proof dish. Add the grapes. Sprinkle with the fat and juices from the sauté pan and cook, uncovered, in a hot oven for 5 minutes. Add the stock and brandy and return to the oven, covered, for a further 5 minutes or until tender.

4 Quails
1 tablespoon butter
4 thin rashers of fat bacon
4 vine leaves
4 oz. green grapes, peeled and seeded
4 tablespoons game stock
2 tablespoons brandy

Menu

Melon

—

Scampi A La Veiner

—

Casserole of Quail
Grapes
Parsley Boiled Potatoes
Braised Celery
Peas

—

Compote of Pears
Fresh Cream, Chocolate Sauce

—

Cheese – Biscuits

—

Coffee   Sweetmeats

Chilled Honeydew Melon

Method

1. Cut melon into 4 even size pieces (depending on size) and remove seeds.
2. Using a knife, cut segments of melon flesh away from the peel. Retain attractively in the "shells".
3. Cut rings of orange (leave rind on), twist and thread on 4 cocktail sticks. Pierce cherry on top of each.

Serving

On individual plates with ginger and castor sugar served separately. For sheer extravagance a teaspoonful of Grand Marnier can be poured over the top of the flesh of each piece of melon. Serve very cold.

1 ripe melon
Ginger
Castor sugar
4 cherries
4 thin rings orange

Scampi à la Veiner

Method

1. Peel and dice onion very finely.
2. Peel and slice mushrooms. If white button, do not peel.
3. Dice tomatoes — sieve to remove seeds — reserve juice and flesh.
4. Melt butter in pan. Gently sauté (5 minutes) onion. Do not brown.

8 oz. (200g.) scampi or prawns
1 oz. (25g.) butter
3 medium sized tomatoes
3 tablespoonsful double cream
1 onion
6 oz. (150g.) mushrooms
1 glass white wine
Salt, pepper

5. Add scampi and mushrooms. Sauté further 5 minutes. Lastly, add tomato flesh and juice and cook 3–4 minutes.
6. Add wine, stir, remove from heat, stir in cream.
   Serve hot garnished with parsley. Buttered brown bread is handed round separately.

Compôte of Fresh Pears

Method
1. Peel pears, halve, then using a teaspoon scoop out core of each.
2. Dissolve sugar in water and lemon juice over low heat, bring to boil, add pears and simmer until fruit is soft – about 15 minutes.
3. Pour pears and juice into serving dish. Wash grapes, cut in half lengthways, de-seed and add to pears.
4. Cool and chill before serving with cream or chocolate sauce.

4 fairly firm fresh pears
6 oz. (150g.) castor sugar
½ lb. (200g.) green grapes
¼ pt. (125ml.) water
Juice of 1 lemon

Chocolate Sauce

Method
Melt syrup, broken chocolate and butter in pan. Blend cornflour with sugar and milk and add, stirring all the time. Simmer 2 to 3 minutes, then stir in raisins.

2 teaspoonsful sugar
3–4 oz. (approx. 100g.) dark chocolate
1 tablespoonful syrup
4 level teaspoonsful cornflour
2 tablespoonsful butter
½ cup milk
1 oz. (25g.) raisins (optional)

Roast Quail

Clean and truss the birds, brush with melted butter and wrap around with fat bacon. Place in a casserole with melted butter and cook in a hot oven for 20 minutes. Baste frequently. The flavour is improved if vine leaves are also wrapped around the bird.

Grilled Quail

Split the birds in half and season with salt and black pepper. Brush with melted butter and wrap in thickly buttered cooking foil. Grill for about 8 minutes on each side. Serve on croûtons of fried bread and garnish with fried bread.

Rabbit

Rabbits are at their best between 3 and 4 months old. At this age they are plump and have plenty of white fat around the kidneys. The eyes should be bright, the feet flexible and the claws smooth. The ears of a young rabbit will tear easily and the lower jaw will yield to pressure between the finger and thumb. Rabbits are paunched immediately they are killed, and hung, head down, for 4 to 5 days. Young rabbits are suitable for roasting, but older animals should be used for a civet or stew. Rabbits are skinned in the same way as hares.

Roast Rabbit

Skin the rabbit, wash it thoroughly and dry it. Stuff and truss the rabbit. Tie the strips of fat bacon over the back of the rabbit. Cover with greased paper and tin foil. Heat the dripping in a roasting tin, put in the rabbit, roast in a hot oven for one hour. Baste every 10 minutes as rabbit flesh is very dry. Remove the paper and bacon, sprinkle a little flour over the rabbit, baste well and return to the oven for 10 minutes to brown. Place on a serving dish and keep warm. Remove skewers and string. Drain all but 1 dessertspoon of fat from the roasting tin, add the remainder of the flour and cook till brown. Take off heat and gradually stir in the stock. Boil up for 5 minutes, adjust the seasoning and pour into gravy boat. Bacon rolls and a sharp jelly or bread sauce are served with roast rabbit.

1 young rabbit
½ lb. fat bacon strips
½ pt. stock
Seasoning
Forcemeat
½ lb. dripping
1 tablespoon flour

Menu

Soused Herrings

—

Leek and Carrot Soup

—

Roast Rabbit
Game Chips
Broccoli, Braised Celery
Cauliflower Sprigs

—

Lemon Cheese Cake

—

Cheese — Biscuits

—

Coffee   Sweetmeats

Soused Herrings

This recipe is not heavily spiced and so produces a mild delicate flavour.

4 herrings
1 medium sized onion
Salt, pepper
1 full teaspoon pickling spice
Malt vinegar
Water
1 bay leaf
1 red apple (not peeled)

Method
1. Light oven Reg. 5 or 375°F (190°C)
2. Wash herrings, cut off heads, tails and fins. Wash under running water and wipe with kitchen paper. Split the herrings open and remove guts. Rinse again. Run finger down backbone and remove. All this the fishmonger will do if asked.
3. Lay the piece of fish out flat, fleshy side uppermost.
4. Place rings of onion on each and season with salt and pepper. Roll up tightly from the neck end and secure in position with cocktail stick or cotton.
5. Pack herrings side by side in suitable dish. Half fill with equal quantities of vinegar and cold water and add bay leaf.
6. Place lid on dish, bake 45 minutes.
7. Remove from dish and allow to go cold.

Serving
When cold cut each roll into two and pierce with a clean cocktail stick. Per person: place 2 small rolls on a lettuce leaf and garnish with a sprig of parsley and a quarter slice tomato and apple. Thin slices of brown bread and butter should be to hand.

Leek and Carrot Soup

Method
1. Prepare carrots and slice. Leaving about 1″ (2.5cm.) green on leeks, cut in half and wash very well, then shred. Peel and dice onion.
2. Melt butter in pan, add vegetables and sauté about 10 minutes. Add stock and seasoning and simmer about $1\frac{1}{2}$ hours.
3. Sieve or liquidise, return to pan and heat. Before serving stir in cream.

1 lb. carrots
3 large leeks
1 onion
$\frac{1}{4}$ pt. (125ml.) single cream or rich milk
2 oz. (50g.) butter
2 pts. stock (made with 2 chicken stockcubes)
Salt, pepper

Lemon Cheesecake

Method
1. Crush biscuits into crumbs between paper. Mix with melted butter and press into a 7″ (17.5cm.) tin. Place in refrigerator.
2. Dissolve jelly in $\frac{1}{4}$ pt. (125ml.) boiling water and when cool blend in cream cheese, lemon juice and finely grated rind and cream or evaporated milk.
3. Pour on top of biscuit crumbs and return to refrigerator to chill. Can be decorated with cherries etc., or fresh fruit just before serving.

2 oz. (50g.) butter
4 oz. (100g.) semi-sweet biscuits
Filling
1 lemon jelly
8 oz. (200g.) creamcheese
Rind and juice 1 lemon
$\frac{1}{4}$ pt. (125ml.) cream or small tin evaporated milk

Note
To facilitate the removal of the cheese cake from the tin before serving, a piece of greased paper can be placed on the greased bottom of the tin before pressing in the biscuit crumbs.

Sauté Rabbit

Joint the rabbit and rub the joints with seasoning. Heat the butter in a heavy frying pan. Brown the rabbit joints, then turn the heat very low and cook gently for about half an hour, turning the joints frequently. Place the joints on a serving dish and keep hot. Sauté the chopped shallots in the frying pan, adding more butter if necessary, until they are soft but not coloured. Add the chives and wine. Simmer for 10 minutes. Adjust the seasoning and pour over the rabbit joints. Garnish with lemon slices.

1 young rabbit
8 shallots
1 glass white wine
Seasoning
6 oz. butter
2 tablespoons chopped chives
1 lemon

Rabbit Chasseur

Cut the rabbit into suitably sized pieces. Heat the butter in a heavy pan and sauté the rabbit pieces and chopped shallots until nicely browned. Work the flour into the fat in the pan, add the purée and, gradually, the wine and stock. Season and simmer gently for an hour. Slice the mushrooms, sauté them lightly in butter and add to the rabbit. Simmer for a further 10 minutes. Place the rabbit pieces in a serving dish. Reduce the sauce to a syrupy consistency, adjust the seasoning and pour over the rabbit. Garnish with the chopped parsley.

1 young rabbit
4 oz. clarified butter
1 dessertspoon flour
⅓ pt. stock
Chopped parsley
2 glasses white wine
2 oz. shallots
1 teaspoon tomato purée
6 oz. mushrooms
Seasoning

Rabbit à la Espãgnole

Joint the rabbit and retain the liver. Heat the butter in a heavy pan and stiffen the sliced liver for a moment or two. Lift it out and brown the rabbit joints. Chop the onion, quarter the tomatoes, and add them, together with the red wine, crushed garlic, red pepper, bouquet garni and seasoning to the rabbit. Add enough stock to just cover the meat. Cover the pan and simmer gently for an hour. Pound the liver and add this to the pan. Cook for 20 minutes with the lid off. If the sauce is not thick enough add a little beurre manie. Remove the bouquet garni and serve.

1 rabbit and liver
3 tomatoes
2 glasses red wine
2 cloves garlic
Bouquet Garni
4 oz. butter
2 onions
Stock
1 red pepper (small) or
$\frac{1}{4}$ teaspoon cayenne pepper
Seasoning

Rabbit Pie

Cut the rabbit into joints or pieces and the ham or steak into large dice. Chop the onion. Heat the butter in a heavy pan and fry the meat and onion until nicely brown. Sprinkle with salt and pepper and add the stock. Simmer gently for 45 minutes. Leave until cold. Fill a pie dish with the meat and stock. Place a funnel in the centre of the dish and cover with pastry. Bake at 400° for about 1 hour, brush over with a little milk and return to the oven for a further 10 minutes.

1 rabbit
$\frac{1}{2}$ lb. flaky pastry
1 large onion
Seasoning
$\frac{1}{2}$ lb. ham, bacon or steak
3 oz. butter
$\frac{1}{2}$ pt. stock

Snipe

At their best October to December. Allow one bird per person. Snipe are usually hung until rather 'high', although this is a matter of taste. Snipe are dressed without being drawn, care being taken in the plucking as the skin is very tender; the gizzard is removed and the eyes removed from the head which is skinned and left on the bird. The beak is used instead of a skewer for trussing the bird.

Roast Snipe

Press the legs and wings together, draw the head round and run the beak through where the legs and wings cross. Brush the bird with melted butter and tie a piece of fat bacon round each bird. Place in a casserole with some melted butter, season and baste with butter. Cook in a hot oven for 12 minutes, basting frequently. Serve on croûtons of fried bread. The snipe may be sprinkled with a dessertspoonful of brandy. The croûtons may be spread with chicken livers, pâté or foie gras. The birds are garnished with watercress and lemon butterflies and served with a good gravy.

Snipe Souvaroff

Stuff the snipe with a stuffing made of foie gras and truffles seasoned and moistened with brandy. Cook in butter containing chopped truffles. Serve with a giblet and madeira sauce.

Madeira Sauce

Fry bacon and shallots in butter until golden brown. Add the flour, brown and cook out. Add purée, mushroom stalks, stock, seasoning and simmer for 15 minutes. Add herbs and Madeira and simmer for another 5 minutes. Strain and simmer until correct consistency, about 3 minutes.

½ oz. butter
3 shallots chopped finely
2 oz. bacon chopped finely
1 level dessertspoon flour
6 or 8 mushroom stalks
1 teaspoon tomato purée
½ pt. stock
1 teaspoon mixed herbs
Seasoning
1 sherry glass Madeira

Venison

To be correct only the meat of the red deer is venison, but most people use the term venison to cover the meat of the roe, fallow and sika deer. The best joint for roasting is the haunch. Venison lacks natural fat and must, therefore, always be kept moist when cooking. Very young animals need not be marinated but it is advisable to marinate meat from any animal over the age of eighteen months.

Venison liver is a great delicacy and is usually considered one of the stalker's perks. It is removed from the animal as soon as it has been killed and fried and eaten as soon as possible.

Roast Haunch of Venison

Marinate the haunch for 24 hours. Remove from marinade and rub all over with oil. Dab all over with pats of butter and wrap around with the fat bacon. Smear a sheet of greaseproof paper on both sides with olive oil. Wrap the meat in the greased paper. Place in a covered roasting tin, or wrap in foil. Roast in a hot oven (500°) for 15 minutes, then reduce the heat to 300° allowing 25 minutes per pound. Baste frequently. 15 minutes before the end of the cooking time, unwrap the haunch and remove the bacon strips. Sprinkle flour over the top of the haunch, baste well and return to a hot oven for 10-15 minutes. Place haunch on serving dish and pour off all but 1 tablespoon of fat from the roasting tin. Add the flour and cook till brown. Remove from heat and gradually add the burgundy and lemon, or orange juice. Bring to the boil, stirring all the time, and simmer for a few minutes. Adjust the seasoning. Serve redcurrant jelly with the venison.

Haunch of venison
Marinade
¾ lb. fat bacon strips
¼ pt. burgundy
Seasoning
½ lb. butter
Olive oil
1 tablespoon flour
Juice of half a lemon or orange

The above cooking time is for red deer. Roe deer will only require 15 minutes per pound using the same method.

Menu

Pamplemousse Jamaica

—

Vichysoisse Soup

—

Roast Haunch of Venison
French Fried Potatoes
Broccoli Spears
Cauliflower, Braised Leeks

—

Orange Mousse

—

Cheese — Biscuits

—

Coffee   Sweetmeats

Pamplemousse Jamaica

Method

1. Cut grapefruits in half and with a grapefruit knife release each segment.
2. Run 1 to 2 teaspoonsful rum over the surface of each ½ grapefruit and sprinkle with brown sugar.
3. Heat under a hot grill until sugar dissolves, and serve hot with a cherry on top — half to each person.

2 Grapefruits
Brown sugar
Rum
4 marachino cherries

VichySoisse- Leek and Potato Soup

Method

1. Wash very thoroughly stems of leeks (discard green leaves), shred. Peel and finely dice onion.
2. Sauté leeks and onion in melted butter in a covered pan for about 5 minutes. Do not brown.
3. Add diced potatoes, stock and seasoning. Simmer gently 30–45 minutes or until vegetables are soft.
4. Sieve or liquidise — check seasoning — add cream.
5. Serve hot sprinkled with chopped chives or parsley.

¾ lb. (375g.) approx. white part leeks
1 onion
1 oz. (25g.) butter
¾ lb. (375g.) potatoes
1½ pts. (750ml.) stock or 2 pts water and 2 chicken stock cubes
Salt, pepper
¼ pt. single cream or rich milk
Chopped chives or parsley

Orange Mousse

Method

1. Squeeze juice from orange and lemon. Reserve.
2. Measure cold water into a small pan and add gelatine, fruit juices and finely grated rind from orange and lemon.
3. Separate eggs and place yolks in one basin and whites in another.
4. Whisk yolks with 2 oz (50g) of the sugar until pale in colour, then whisk in fruit juice mixture. Set aside, whisking occasionally until mixture is cool but not cold (it will thicken when cold).
5. Whisk egg whites until very thick and fold into yolk mixture when it is slightly thickening, together with remaining 1 oz (25g) castor sugar.
6. Pour into either 1 large or individual dishes and decorate with segments of orange or tangerine or flaked chocolate.

Note

This dish can be made the day before required. The sweet can be served with short bread or meringues.

2 large oranges
½ lemon
3 large eggs
½ oz. (15g.) gelatine – 1 sachet from a box
4 brimming tablespoonfuls cold water
3 oz. (75g.) castor sugar

Braised Venison

Marinate the venison for 2 to 3 days, turning occasionally. Dry the meat and brown all over in hot fat or oil. Slice the onions, carrots and celery, fry gently for 5-10 minutes, and place in the bottom of a casserole. Place the venison on top and add the herbs, marinade, stock and orange peel. Season. Cover the casserole and braise gently in a moderate oven for 2-2½ hours. Baste occasionally. When the venison is cooked, slice and arrange on a serving dish. Strain the liquor from the casserole, reduce a little, and add the orange juice and redcurrant jelly. Thicken with beurre manie. Spoon a little of the sauce over the meat and hand the rest separately.

Haunch or loin of venison
2 onions
4 sticks of celery
Bunch of Fresh herbs or bouquet garni
1 tablespoon redcurrant jelly
Seasoning
Marinade
2 carrots
½ pt. stock
Rind and juice of an orange
Beurre Manie

Venison Stew

Cut the venison into 2 inch cubes and marinate for 6-8 hours. Remove the venison from the marinade and dry. Roll the cubes in seasoned flour. Dice the bacon and sauté until golden. Place in a casserole. Sauté the venison in the bacon fat until brown. Place in casserole. Slice the onions and sauté in the fat until browned. Add to the casserole. Add carrots, herbs, red wine, garlic and seasoning. Cover and cook in a slow oven for 3 hours. Just before serving, stir in the redcurrant jelly.

2 lb. venison
2 onions
½ lb. bacon in a piece
1 teaspoon mixed herbs
½ bottle red wine
Flour
Marinade
4 carrots
5 cloves garlic
1 bay leaf
1 tablespoon redcurrant jelly
Seasoning

Grilled Venison Steaks

After marinating the steaks they may be grilled as for beef steak, but allowing rather longer cooking time. The steaks must be served immediately or they will become tough.

Fried Venison Steaks

After marinating, fry the steaks in butter and a little dry sherry, turning them several times during the cooking period.

Sautéd Venison

Cut the venison into $\frac{3}{4}$-inch thick slices, allowing 1 slice per person. Season and marinate for 36 hours. Heat a large frying pan, and put in enough butter to cover the bottom. Dry the venison slices and put into the fat. Fry over a moderate heat until brown on one side, turn over and brown on the other. This should take about 20 minutes. Turn the heat very low, cover the pan and cook until the meat is tender for approximately a further 20 minutes. Lay the slices, overlapping, down a long serving dish and keep warm. Strain the marinade into the pan and boil briskly. Adjust the seasoning and add the juniper berries. crushed, and the lemon juice. Spoon the sauce over the meat and garnish with lemon butterflies.

Loin or haunch of venison
Butter
Juice of half a lemon
Seasoning
Marinade
6 Juniper berries
Lemon butterflies or slices

Woodcock

At their best October to December. Hang until 'high' to allow it to yield its full flavour, when it is considered by many to be the best eating of all game birds. At one time wood-cock was a breakfast dish and some still enjoy it as such. It may also be served as a 'starter' or a savoury.

Roast Woodcock

Press the legs and wings together, draw the head round and run the beak through where the legs and wings cross. Brush the birds with melted butter and tie a piece of fat bacon round each bird. Place in a casserole with some melted butter, season and baste with butter. Cook in a hot oven for 20-30 minutes, basting frequently. Cut the birds in half and serve on croûtons of fried bread or toast and serve with a clear gravy made from the cook-ing juices and flavoured with a squeeze of lemon. Alternatively, the birds may be wrapped in fat bacon and then placed on a piece of bread which has been fried or toasted on one side, the birds being placed on the un-toasted side so that the juices will run into the bread while roasting.

Menu

Grapefruit Cocktail

—

Danish Plaice

—

Roast Woodcock
Game Chips
Corn On The Cob
Courgettes

—

Pavlova Meringue
Fresh Cream

—

Cheese — Biscuits

—

Coffee   Sweetmeats

Grapefruit Cocktail

To serve 4 persons.

Method

1. Cut grapefruits in half and with a sharp knife loosen each segment and place into a bowl, taking care not to lose any juice.
2. Stir 5 heaped teaspoons castor sugar and 4 teaspoons Crême de Menthe into the grapefruit and stir well to dissolve the sugar and to blend the green colour.
3. Divide the fruit mixture evenly between 4 glasses and chill thoroughly.
   Garnish before serving with a cherry and a sprig of mint.

3 whole grapefruits
Castor sugar
Crême de Menthe (miniature bottle)
Sprigs mint
4 cherries

Danish Plaice with Cucumber Sauce

Method

1. Wipe fish, roll into tight rolls starting at neck end. Secure back with cocktail stick (or tie with cotton).
2. Place fish in buttered casserole dish, season, place little butter on each and bake with lid 20–30 minutes Reg. 5 or 375°F (190°C).

4 small pieces filleted plaice (skinned)
Few Grapes
Butter
Cucumber sauce
½ cucumber
1 oz. (25 g.) butter
1 oz. (25 g.) flour
2–3 tablespoonfuls single cream or top of milk
½ pt. (250 ml.) Milk
Salt, pepper
Lemon juice

Cucumber Sauce

1. Peel cucumber, slice in $\frac{1}{2}$ lengthways, remove seeds, chop flesh.
2. Melt butter in pan, add cucumber, cover with lid and cook very gently about 5 minutes to soften cucumber.
3. Sprinkle in flour and slowly add milk drop by drop, stirring all the time. Season well with salt and pepper.
4. Stirring all the time, bring slowly to boil. Simmer 2 minutes.
5. Remove any pieces of cucumber.
6. When ready to serve add lemon juice to taste. Stir in cream.

Serving

Pour sauce attractively over fish and garnish with parsley and grapes (cut in half lengthways and deseeded). Serve hot.

Pavlova Meringue

Method

1. Cover baking sheet with non-stick paper and draw a 7" (17.5 cm.) circle on top. Light oven Reg. 2 or 300°F or 150°C.
2. Whisk egg whites until standing in peaks and very stiff.
3. Sieve in $\frac{1}{2}$ of sugar, whisking all the time.
4. Sieve in remainder of sugar mixed with cornflour. Add lemon juice or vinegar and stir.
5. Place all of mixture onto 7" (17.5 cm.) circle working up sides to make a small wall.

3 egg whites
6 oz. (150g.) castor sugar
1 rounded and 1 level teaspoonful cornflour
1 teaspoonful lemon juice or white vinegar
Fruit, e.g. peaches
Cream

6. Bake 2nd shelf from the bottom for 1 to 1½ hours. The finished meringue should be crisp on the outside with a marsh mallow centre. Carefully remove from baking sheet, cool, then store in an airtight tin. Serve filled with fruit and cream.

Woodcock à l'Orange

Cook the woodcock in the oven or on a spit, arrange on croûtons spread with the trail. Dilute the pan juices with $\frac{1}{2}$ cup of dry white wine and a few tablespoons of concentrated game stock. Simmer for 5 minutes. Add the juice of one orange, strain, and add the zest of one orange. Blend in a teaspoonful of butter. Pour this sauce over the woodcock and garnish with sections of orange.

Woodcock à la Fine Champagne

Roast the woodcock for 12 minutes. Cut joints in a dish and keep warm. Chop up the intestines as finely as possible and press the carcase to squeeze out as much blood and juice as possible. Add the intestines to this liquid, pour over a small glass of brandy and flame. Add a teaspoonful of concentrated game stock, a dash of lemon juice and a little cayenne pepper. Pour the sauce over the birds in the serving dish.

Galantine of Game

Slice the breasts off the birds and put on one side. Remove the rest of the meat, mince and mix with the pork and veal. Place the carcases in a pan with the vegetables, parsley and seasoning. Bring to the boil and simmer for two hours. Strain the stock and reduce to about a pint. Line a terrine or earthenware casserole first with some of the breast, then with the forcemeat, seasoning between each layer. Put the terrine in a tin of hot water and cook in a medium oven for an hour. Heat the liquid and dissolve the gelatine in this. Allow to cool a little, add the wine and pour over the cooked gelatine. When set, turn out on to a serving dish and garnish with the rest of the aspic, chopped, with lettuce and tomato.

1 cooked grouse
$\frac{1}{4}$ lb. minced pork
$\frac{1}{2}$ pt. red wine
1 onion
Parsley
1 cooked pheasant
$\frac{1}{4}$ lb. minced veal
$\frac{1}{2}$ oz. gelatine
1 carrot
Seasoning

Terrine of Game

Heat the butter in a strong pan and brown the birds. Add the veal, cut in large pieces, the stock, cloves and peppercorns and seasoning. Simmer for 1¾ hours. Remove the birds and cut the meat into pieces. Remove the veal. Replace the bones in the stock, simmer and reduce to 2 pints. Strain the stock and leave to cool. Skim off the fat. Dissolve the aspic powder and stir into the stock. Add the wine. Arrange the cut meat into a terrine dish with slices of hard-boiled egg. Pour over the aspic when on the point of settling. Leave to set. Turn out on to a serving dish and garnish with watercress or mustard and cress and slices of pimento or stuffed olive.

1 pheasant
3 pt. game stock
½ tablespoon salt
3 cloves
2 hard-boiled eggs
2 partridge
2 oz. butter
3 tablespoons powdered aspic
8 white peppercorns
¾ lb. shin of veal
½ pt. white wine

Stuffings

Onion

Either a shallot for a small Teal or $\frac{1}{2}$ a whole onion for a Widgeon will often improve the flavour particularly in hard weather.

Orange or Tangerine

An orange cut into 2 or 4 sections lengthwise slips into the abdominal cavity and is a welcome variation to improve the flavour.

Sage and Onion

Probably the most usual stuffing and one of the best.

Skin the onion and place in cold water—bring to the boil—discard the water and place in cold again. Boil and simmer until tender. Mix the chopped onion with white bread-crumbs, chopped suet, salt and pepper and 3 or 4 sage leaves which have been blanched and chopped, a nut of butter and an egg to bind the stuffing. This stuffing can be obtained in a packet for use in emergencies.

Apple and Sausage

Lightly fry sausage meat, just brown sliced apple in the fat and mix with 1 tablespoon of sugar, a dash of cinnamon and 2 tablespoons of brandy.

Apple and Prune
1 lb. sliced raw apples and a number of whole soaked prunes. Particularly good with goose.

Apple and Raisin
A combination of raw apples with raisins, shredded suet, white breadcrumbs and an egg, seasoned to taste.

Parsnips or Artichokes
Either of these roots make a change if chopped and put in the birds with a good sized knob of butter.

Espagnole Sauce

Dice the bacon and vegetables finely. Heat the oil and add the bacon and vegetables. Cook slowly for about 15 minutes, stirring occasionally. Add the flour and cook slowly for a further 15 minutes, still stirring. The flour should be golden brown. Remove from heat and add $1\frac{3}{4}$ pints of stock, the white wine, mushroom peelings and bouquet garni. Bring to the boil and simmer for 30 minutes. Add the remainder of the stock, cool and skim. Reduce the sherry to half and add to the sauce. Adjust the seasoning.

2 tablespoons oil
1 carrot
2 tablespoons flour
1 bouquet garni
2 tablespoons tomato purée
1 wineglass white wine
2 oz. bacon
2 oz. mushroom peelings
1 onion
2 pt. good stock
1 clove garlic
Seasoning
1 glass sherry

Beurre Manie

This is a liaison used to thicken sauces, etc., and is especially useful where the quantity of liquid is unknown.

Take two-thirds butter to one-third flour and work together into a paste, break into small pieces and roll each of these into a ball. Add these balls, one at a time, to the contents of the pan or casserole, draw off the heat, stir or shake the pan gently taking care not to break the meat. The butter melts and draws the flour into the liquid. Reboil and, if still not thick enough, repeat the process.

Demi-Glâce

Dice the vegetables finely. Heat the oil and add the vegetables. Cook the vegetables on a low heat until barely coloured. Stir in the flour and cook slowly, stirring, until a good brown colour. Remove from heat and add $\frac{3}{4}$ pint of stock and all other ingredients. Bring to the boil and simmer for 25 minutes. Add the remainder of the stock, cool and skim. Strain the sauce and adjust the seasoning.

3 tablespoons oil
1 small onion
2 oz. mushroom peelings
1 teaspoon tomato pureé
1 pt. good brown stock
1 small carrot
1 small stick celery
1 tablespoon flour
Bouquet Garni
Seasoning

Clarified Butter

The object of clarifying butter is to take away the milk solids and salt in the butter. This produces a clear fat, free from all moisture, which, when heated, is not so inclined to burn as unclarified butter and therefore a greater temperature can be reached. It also gives an especially good golden colour.

To clarify: Heat $\frac{3}{4}$ lb. butter gently in a pan until it foams well. Cook for another $\frac{1}{2}$ minute, skim and pour off into a bowl. Do not allow the butter to brown. When cold all the sediments will have fallen to the bottom and this must be scraped away. 4 oz. butter will yield a bare 3 oz. when clarified.

Marinade for Venison or Hare

Put all ingredients in a pan, bring to the boil and simmer for 10 minutes. Leave to cool and pour over the raw meat. The meat may be marinated for 24-28 hours, turning the meat over in the marinade occasionally.

N.B. When marinating use a glass or china dish. NOT an enamel or metal one.

½ pt. oil
1 pt. burgundy type cooking wine
2 sticks celery
Bouquet Garni
A clove of garlic
A bunch of parsley stalks
½ pt. wine vinegar
1 onion, sliced
6 crushed juniper berries if available
Sprig of Rosemary
Sprig of orange rind

Sweetmeats

Petits Foius

Method

1. Either place rice paper on baking sheet or grease a tray.
2. Mix together ground almonds and sugar.
3. Whisk egg white until stiff and mix into almonds together with almond essence.
4. Pipe or place teaspoonsful of the mixture onto rice paper. Decorate each with a small piece cherry or angelica. Mixture can also be piped into $1\frac{1}{2}$ inch (4cm) fingers.
5. Bake Reg 6 or 400°F (200°C) for about 10 minutes, taking care not to overbake — should be just coloured.
6. When cool the tiny fingers can be dipped each end in melted chocolate. Serve as an accompaniment to coffee with pieces of crystallised ginger.

3 oz. (75g.) ground almonds
1½ oz. (45g.) castor sugar
2 oz. (50g.) plain chocolate
(optional)
Few drops almond essence
Rice paper (optional)
1 egg white
Decoration
Glacé cherries
Angelica

Juices

Tomato
Serve chilled with Worcester Sauce. Slices of cucumber can be twisted and pressed on cocktail sticks across top of glasses.

The glasses for the fruit juices can be "frosted" by damping rims with water then dipping in sugar and allowing to dry. Pieces of fruit can be cut into rings, slit $\frac{1}{2}$ across the centre and twisted to sit on the rims of each glass. Serve chilled.

Tomato
Orange
Grapefruit

Chocolate Truffles

Method
1. Break chocolate into pan, add butter and melt. Add rum.
2. Rub cake into fine crumbs, add icing sugar and mix.
3. Pour melted chocolate and butter into crumbs and mix well together.
4. Form into small balls and roll in vermicilli while still warm. Place in sweet cases — truffles harden on cooling.

Serve as an accompaniment to coffee, perhaps with pieces of crystallized ginger.

4 oz. (100g.) dark chocolate
2 oz. (50g.) butter
4 oz. (100g.) plain cake crumbs
Rum essence or 2 tablespoonful rum
Approx. 2 oz. (50g.) chocolate vermicilli
4 oz. (100g.) icing sugar
Small sweet cases

Tossed Salad

Method

1. Wash lettuce leaves, dry and leave whole. Place in salad bowl. Wash and cut into small pieces spring onion or onion. Mix altogether, adding cucumber cut into cubes.
2. Prepare French Dressing. Place all ingredients into screw-topped jar and shake well, salt first adding a little to salad ingredients — just enough to make leaves glisten. Toss together.

Note
Only toss the salad just before it is required.

1 Dutch or hot house type lettuce
1 piece cucumber
1 spring onion with green t
or 1 very small onion
French dressing
1 tablespoonful vinegar
3 tablespoonsful corn or salad oil
2 teaspoonsful cold water
Pinch mustard, pinch ugar, pinch salt, pinch pepper.

To Braise Celery and Leeks

Method

1. Wash celery hearts or leeks very well indeed.
2. Peel and dice carrot, onion and swede. Place in pan.
3. Lay celery or leeks on top of vegetables, add stock and bay leaf. Cover with buttered foil and lid. Simmer about 30 minutes.
4. Carefully lift out celery or leeks and place at bottom of buttered serving dish. Strain liquor from pan and reduce by boiling to half, then pour over celery or leeks. Cover with foil and bake about 20 minutes (350°F, 160°C Reg. 4).
5. Scatter chopped parsley over the top and serve from dish.

Celery hearts or 4 leeks
1 carrot
1 onion
1 bay leaf
Salt, pepper
Small piece swede (optiona'
Stock
½ pt. boiling water
1 beef cube